Thirtysix.org

Haggadah shel Pesach
The Wise Son Says…

ISBN 9798328919937

© 2024 by Thirtysix.org. All rights reserved. No part of this publication may be reproduced in any form, stored in a retrieval system, or transmitted in any form or by any means, whether electronic, mechanical, recording, by photocopying, or otherwise, if the intended use is not consistent with the intention of the publisher and the copyright holder. Failure to comply with the above is a violation of international copyright laws.

Please send corrections to: pinchasw@thirtysix.org.

Published by:
Thirtysix.org & Shaarnun Productions
22 Yitzchak Road
Telzstone, Kiryat Yearim, Israel
9083800

Sneider Family Haggadah

Iluy Nishmas Yitzhak Moshe ben Yaakov z"l
& Tzivia Bas Chaim z"l

We are very pleased to make a dedication in this recent and important contribution to the growing collection of *Haggados Shel Pesach*. We pray that it enrich the Seder experience for countless Jews around the world for years to come, *b"H*, and bring great merit to all those fortunate to be a part of its coming to light. We thank Rabbi Winston for the opportunity to be a part of his work on behalf of *Klal Yisroel*.

Chaim, Chava, Shoshana, Shalom Gershon & Zvi Binyamin Beliak
Toronto, Canada

Thank you Rabbi Winston for all of your teachings since you began sharing them. We pray that your *Haggadah* will greatly benefit all those who use it.

Benaim Family
Boca Raton, Florida

Dedicated in loving memory of departed parents and grandparents

Jonathan Straight
Leeds, United Kingdom

Introduction	7
Seder	12
Kadesh	15
Urchatz	23
Karpas	26
Yachatz	29
Maggid	36
Rachtzah	95

Motzi	96
Matzah	97
Marror	101
Korech	105
Shulchan Aruch	107
Tzafun	109
Barech	113
Hallel	126
Nirtzah	149
Zemiros	152

Introduction

*I*t is a curious thing. Each year millions of Jews around the world sit down to make a *Pesach Seder* to commemorate an event that much of the world thinks never happened, including the majority of Jews. But, we make one anyhow, including Jews who question the origin of this tradition.

We are not the only people to do this. Various religions and cultures also continue to celebrate questionable historic events, the spirits of which tend to be contradicted by present-day lifestyles. It's the power of tradition that keeps alive what for many died long ago.

Hypocrisy? Sometimes. Perhaps this is what bothers the *Evil Son*, the Evil Son and main antagonist in the *Haggadah*. He's the one who has the gumption to ask, *"What does this service mean to you?"*

As the *Bais HaLevi*[1] explains, it's not that the *Evil Son* disagrees that the *Pesach* Offering once had meaning. A lamb

---

[1] Rabbi Yosef Dov[a] Soloveitchik (1820–1892) was a rabbi of Brisk (*Brisker Rebbe*), and the author of *Bais HaLevi* by which name he is better known.

Introduction

back then was an Egyptian god, and we had to break away from that to become worthy of redemption. "But who," the *Evil Son* asks, "makes a god out of a lamb today?"[2]

Though we "break his teeth" for asking his question and chastise him saying, "Had you been there, you would not have been redeemed!" the truth is, his question is a good one. In fact, it is one that the *Haggadah* each year asks all of us to answer by the end of the evening. The right answer is not only *liberating*, it is *freedom* itself.

Because the problem with the *Evil Son* is not his question, but his answer. For him, the question *is* the answer, because for him it is rhetorical: this service may have made sense back in the days of leaving Egypt, but today it is meaningless.

For that, we break his teeth and rap his knuckles. But how do we know for sure that the *Evil Son* would not have left Egypt had he been there? Would he not have had a different perspective then while actually going through redemption?

Not really. It is his approach to truth in general that reveals his Four-Fifths mentality. Had he been there, the *Evil Son*

---

[2] *Haggadah Shel Bais HaLevi.* Hence, when the *Haggadah* says, "to you, and not to him," the "him" he refers is really "Him," that is, God Himself. That is, the *Evil Son* doesn't just say the *mitzvah* has no meaning for him, but for God as well.

Introduction

would have been part of the 12 million Jews who died during the Plague of Darkness for not wanting to leave Egypt.[3] Despite what they witnessed, they chose to remain in Egypt because they did not get the message of the *Pesach* Offering.

Sure, we no longer worship Egyptian gods, and therefore no longer have to parade through the streets with a lamb, an Egyptian deity, to prove our loyalty to God. But that is not the entire reason for the *Pesach* Offering. The *Pesach* Offering is always relevant, even long after the Exodus is but a distant memory.

And before it as well. The *Midrash* says that Adam *HaRishon* told his two sons, Kayin and Hevel, to bring their offering on the fourteenth of *Nissan*, the destined night for the *Pesach* Offering by the future Jewish people.[4] The *Bais HaLevi* says that our forefather Avraham was already eating *matzah* on the fifteenth of *Nissan*, hundreds of years before Egyptian exile even began.

If so, the question becomes: Do we eat *matzah* because there wasn't enough time to bake bread when leaving Egypt? Or was there not enough time to bake bread so that we would eat *matzah* each year on *Pesach*? Was leaving in haste

---

[3] *Rashi, Shemos* 13:8; *Sanhedrin* 111a.
[4] *Pirkei d'Rebi Eliezer,* Ch. 21.

9

Introduction

—*b'chipazon*—incidental or intentional?[5]

Contrary to the *Evil Son's* way of thinking, *mitzvos* are eternal. They are beyond everyday reality. They are not circumstantial, though specific circumstances may have led to their introduction, as in the case of the exodus from Egypt and the *Pesach* Offering. If anything, the *mitzvos* make the specific outcomes possible, such as the Exodus in Moshe's time, as they will the leaving of exile in our time.

It is the *Chacham*—Wise Son—in each generation who understands this. He might be part of the evolving world, but he also lives above it. While the *Evil Son* thinks that the modern world is where it is at, and that the Torah world is antiquated, the *Wise Son* knows the opposite is true. From the *Wise Son's* perspective, it is the modern world that is dated, and the Torah world that is eternal. Hence, the *Haggadah's* response to his question: You, in turn, must teach him the laws of *Pesach*...

Wait, that's it? That's the *Wise Son's* entire reward for being on the right side of the argument? Absolutely. Unlike the *Evil Son, halachah* (Jewish law) for the *Wise Son* is not just restrictions to keep a Jew in spiritual line. It is the path to true freedom, designed by God to help a person overcome in-

---

[5] *You must eat it b'chipazon—in haste...* (*Shemos* 12:11)

Introduction

stinctual behavior that overrides the will of the soul.

In fact, it is one of the greatest ironies of life how people think they are free when they are in fact slaves to their *yetzer haras*.[6] *Mitzvos,* and the *halachos* for properly implementing them, are the only true defense a person has against their *yetzer hara* and the true freedom it stifles. Seeing that the *Wise Son* has bought into that truth, we further supply him with the means to achieve it.

So what's it going to be, the *Wise Son's* idea of freedom, or the *Evil Son's*? That is the question the *Haggadah* poses to *all* of us each year we sit down to make a *Seder*. The rest of the evening is to decide for ourselves which path we want to follow, as the prophet said:

Who is wise and will understand these, discerning and will know them; for the ways of God are straight, and the righteous will walk in them, and the rebellious will stumble on them. (Hoshea 14:10)

In closing, it is more practical to read the commentary in advance of the *Seder*, and underline particular points to bring up during the *Seder*. The night is not timeless for everyone at the *Seder*, and patience varies from person to person.

---

[6] The evil inclination, our bodily instinct to satisfy material desires, usually at the cost of spiritual growth.

Seder

קַדֵּשׁ. וּרְחַץ. כַּרְפַּס. יַחַץ. מַגִּיד.
רָחְצָה. מוֹצִיא מַצָּה. מָרוֹר. כּוֹרֵךְ.
שֻׁלְחָן עוֹרֵךְ. צָפוּן. בָּרֵךְ. הַלֵּל.
נִרְצָה.

WHEN WAS THE last time anyone sang a table of contents? That is the way many families begin their *Pesach Seder* each year. Why, and why is it called a *Seder* at all?

The Torah says:

The earth was tohu vavohu—null and void, and there was darkness upon the face of the deep, and the Spirit of God hovered above the water. God said, "Let there be light!" and there was light. (Bereishis 1:2-3)

The creation of light did not only illuminate a very dark world. It was the first step towards ending the *tohu*—chaos—of the first day of Creation, and each subsequent act of creating added to that. By Day Six and the creation of man, all that remained to complete the process was to not eat from the *Aitz HaDa'as Tov v'Ra*, the Tree of Knowledge of Good and

Seder

Evil.

Had Adam *HaRishon* complied, he would have banished chaos from Creation completely and *Yemos HaMoshiach*, the Messianic Era, would have begun. He didn't, and instead increased the chaos in Creation, ending paradise and leaving his descendants to struggle against the chaos of history.

History therefore is meant to be the *tikun*—rectification—of this, which is why, the *Gemora* says, the Torah was given:

Reish Lakish said: "What is the meaning of: '*And there was evening and there was morning, the sixth day—HaShishi*' (*Bereishis* 1:31)? Why [is it not written *shishi* only? Why] do I require the extra *Heh* [which is not used for any of the other days]? It teaches that The Holy One, Blessed is He, established a condition with Creation and said: 'If the Jewish people accept the Torah [on the sixth day of *Sivan* in 2,448 years], you will [be able to continue to] exist; and if they do not accept it, I will return you to the state of *tohu vavohu*—chaos and disorder.'" (*Shabbos* 88a)

This leads us to the answer of another important question about which we should remind ourselves every day: Why did God overtly step into history, suppress the laws of physics, and break the laws of free will to save the Jewish people? This is also something that many have come to take for granted.

Seder

The prophet Yeshayahu said it the clearest:

*I am God; I called you for righteousness and I will strengthen your hand; and I formed you, and I made you for a people's covenant, for **a light to nations**. (Yeshayahu 42:6)*

As we saw on the first day of Creation, it is light that brings order to chaos. Without light, there can be no order. Each year the Jewish people sit down and maker a *Seder* to remind us that we were redeemed from slavery for a specific mission: to bring the light of Torah to the world and order to Creation.

But it is clear from history that what God calls order and what man calls order can be very different. Historically, man's attempt at order has often resulted in chaos, which brings us to the next part of the *Seder*: *Kadesh*.

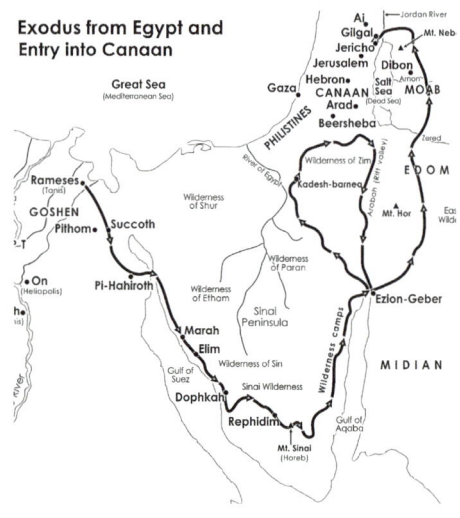

14

Kadesh

THE FOUR CUPS of wine correspond to the four terms of redemption in the Torah, derived from these verses:

*Therefore, say to the Children of Israel, "I am God, and I will take you out (**vehotzeisi**) from under the burdens of the Egyptians, and I will save you (**vehitzalti**) from their labor, and I will redeem you (**vega'alti**) with an outstretched arm and with great judgments. And I will take you (**velakachti**) to Me as a people, and I will be a God to you, and you will know that I am God your God, Who has brought you out from under the burdens of the Egyptians." (Shemos 6:6-7)*

Each word represents a different stage in the redemption process from Egypt.[1] The first term (*vehotzeisi*) refers to the

---

[1] *Aderes Eliyahu, VaAira* 6:6.

Kadesh

end of the labor, the second (*vehitzalti*) to the end of all oppression, the third (*vega'alti*) to the actual leaving of Egypt, and the fourth (*velakachti*) to the receiving of the Torah. In a more general sense, however, each stage of the redemption process can be applied on a personal level as well.

Since this is the first cup, one should have intention for the first terms, *vehotzeisi*—I will take you out.

One of the most important differences between human beings and animals is the ability to distinguish between the holy and the profane. This is what allows a person to strive for spiritual excellence and have a relationship with God:

God spoke to Moshe, saying: "Speak to all the congregation of the Children of Israel, and say to them, 'You shall be holy, for I, God your God, am holy.'" (Vayikra 19:1-2)

If a person loses this ability, they lose their Godliness and descend to the level of *Dalet-Mem* of "Adam," the level of the "*chamor*—donkey," which cannot make such distinctions.[2] They descend to the lowest level of spiritual impurity, as did the Jewish people in Egypt, making them completely material.

Adam—man—is spelled *Aleph-Dalet-Mem*. *Aleph* is the

---

[2] This is explained in more detail in *Maggid*.

Kadesh

number one, and similar to the word *aluph*, which means "chief." Therefore, *Aleph* alludes to God, and comprised of two *Yuds* and a *Vav*, it has a total *gematria* of 26, the same *gematria* as the *Shem Hovayah*, God's four letter Ineffable Name.[3] An *Aleph* even points Heavenward.

Therefore, the *Aleph* of *Adam* represents the Godly part within man, the *soul*. The *Dalet-Mem* spells *dahm*—blood, the symbol of man's physical component (*chomer*), the physical body we have in common with animals. When in balance with the *Aleph*, the letters combine to spell *Adam*, which has the same *gematria* as *geulah*—redemption.

If a person ignores their soul, pursuing the whims of their body, the *Aleph* all but disappears, leaving only the *Dalet-Mem*. Hence, the first of the Ten Plagues was blood, to show the Jewish people what had become of them after 209 years in Egyptian exile. Since the revelation of God increased with each plague, they also strengthened the *Aleph* in the Jewish people until, fully restored, the *Dalet-Mem* became *Aleph-Dalet-Mem*, equalling *geulah*, both in *gematria* and reality.

It is the *Aleph*—the soul—in a person that provides the capacity to be *mavdil*, that is to separate between good and evil, holy and profane, pure and impure. Therefore, the abili-

---

[3] *Osios d'Rebi Akiva*.

Kadesh

ty to make such separations measures the health of the *Aleph* in a person, their level of holiness, and their capacity to relate to God, as it says:

You must therefore distinguish between kosher animals and non-kosher ones, between unclean birds and clean ones… You must be holy to Me, for I, God, am holy, and have separated you from the nations so you can be Mine. (Vayikra 20:25)

Bringing order to chaos depends upon this, as human history makes clear. Too often people do not think deeply enough into ideas to see how they are either similar or different from one another because, on the surface, the opposite seems to be true. Such mistakes have been quite costly, even deadly at times.

We acknowledge this truth and imperative by beginning *Shabbos* and *Yom Tov* with *Kiddush*, a word that also means "separation." It is an important step in the direction of true freedom.

Like royalty, everyone at the Seder should have their cup filled with wine (or grape juice) by another person for each of the four cups.

The person making Kiddush should pick up their cup with both hands, and then hold it in the right hand only (or left hand if left-handed) for the brochah. The cup should sit in

Kadesh

the palm of the hand so the fingers can wrap around the cup from below like rose petals around a flower.[4]

After the brochah, each person should drink the majority of the cup (at least 3.3 fluid ounces) at one time while sitting down and leaning on the left side (women do not have to lean).

If the first night of Pesach is Friday night, then the first cup is also Shabbos Kiddush, a Torah obligation. One should therefore drink at least 4.42 – 5.07 fluid ounces for the first cup only.[5]

Begin here on Shabbos and include the bracketed words:

וַיְהִי עֶרֶב וַיְהִי בֹקֶר יוֹם הַשִּׁשִּׁי:	It was evening and it was day, the sixth day.
וַיְכֻלּוּ הַשָּׁמַיִם וְהָאָרֶץ וְכָל צְבָאָם. וַיְכַל אֱלֹהִים בַּיּוֹם הַשְּׁבִיעִי מְלַאכְתּוֹ אֲשֶׁר עָשָׂה וַיִּשְׁבֹּת בַּיּוֹם הַשְּׁבִיעִי מִכָּל מְלַאכְתּוֹ אֲשֶׁר עָשָׂה. וַיְבָרֶךְ	And the heavens and the earth and all their hosts were completed. And on the seventh day God finished His work which He had made, and He rested on the seventh day from all His

---

[4] *Zohar,* Introduction, Os 2.
[5] *Sefer Kol Dodi,* Siman 2:6.

Kadesh

אֱלֹהִים אֶת יוֹם הַשְּׁבִיעִי וַיְקַדֵּשׁ אֹתוֹ, כִּי בוֹ שָׁבַת מִכָּל מְלַאכְתּוֹ אֲשֶׁר בָּרָא אֱלֹהִים לַעֲשׂוֹת.

work which He had made. And God blessed the seventh day and made it holy, for on it He rested from all His work which God created to do.

Continue here; begin here on a weeknight:

סַבְרִי מָרָנָן וְרַבָּנָן וְרַבּוֹתַי בָּרוּךְ אַתָּה יְיָ אֱלֹהֵינוּ מֶלֶךְ הָעוֹלָם בּוֹרֵא פְּרִי הַגָּפֶן.

Blessed are You, God, our God, King of the universe, Who creates the fruit of the vine.

בָּרוּךְ אַתָּה יְיָ אֱלֹהֵינוּ מֶלֶךְ הָעוֹלָם, אֲשֶׁר בָּחַר בָּנוּ מִכָּל עָם וְרוֹמְמָנוּ מִכָּל לָשׁוֹן וְקִדְּשָׁנוּ בְּמִצְוֹתָיו. וַתִּתֶּן לָנוּ יְיָ אֱלֹהֵינוּ בְּאַהֲבָה (שַׁבָּתוֹת לִמְנוּחָה וּ) מוֹעֲדִים לְשִׂמְחָה, חַגִּים וּזְמַנִּים לְשָׂשׂוֹן, אֶת יוֹם (הַשַּׁבָּת הַזֶּה וְאֶת יוֹם) חַג הַמַּצּוֹת הַזֶּה, זְמַן חֵרוּתֵנוּ (בְּאַהֲבָה), מִקְרָא קֹדֶשׁ, זֵכֶר לִיצִיאַת מִצְרָיִם. כִּי בָנוּ בָחַרְתָּ

Blessed are You, God, our God, King of the universe, Who has chosen us from among all people, and raised us above all languages, and made us holy through His commandments. And You, God, our God, have given us in love (*Shabbos* for rest and) festivals for joy, holidays and times for rejoicing this day (of *Shabbos* and this day) of this holiday of *Matzos*, the time of our freedom (in love) called holy, recalling the departure

20

Kadesh

וְאוֹתָנוּ קִדַּשְׁתָּ מִכָּל הָעַמִּים, (וְשַׁבָּת) וּמוֹעֲדֵי קָדְשֶׁךָ (בְּאַהֲבָה וּבְרָצוֹן,) בְּשִׂמְחָה וּבְשָׂשׂוֹן הִנְחַלְתָּנוּ. בָּרוּךְ אַתָּה יְיָ, מְקַדֵּשׁ (הַשַּׁבָּת וְ) יִשְׂרָאֵל וְהַזְּמַנִּים.

from Egypt. For You have chosen us and sanctified us from all the nations, (and *Shabbos*) and Your holy holidays (in love and desire) in joy and rejoicing You have bequeathed us. Blessed are You, God, Who (sanctifies *Shabbos* and) Israel and the times.

On Motzei Shabbos, a candle with two flames should be lit from an existing flame, and this added. Since it is Yom Tov, the candle should burn out on its own.

בָּרוּךְ אַתָּה יְיָ אֱלֹהֵינוּ מֶלֶךְ הָעוֹלָם, בּוֹרֵא מְאוֹרֵי הָאֵשׁ.

Blessed are You, God, our God, King of the universe, Who creates the lights of fire.

בָּרוּךְ אַתָּה יְיָ אֱלֹהֵינוּ מֶלֶךְ הָעוֹלָם, בּוֹרֵא מְאוֹרֵי הָאֵשׁ. בָּרוּךְ אַתָּה יְיָ אֱלֹהֵינוּ מֶלֶךְ הָעוֹלָם הַמַּבְדִּיל בֵּין קֹדֶשׁ לְחֹל, בֵּין אוֹר לְחֹשֶׁךְ, בֵּין יִשְׂרָאֵל לָעַמִּים, בֵּין יוֹם הַשְּׁבִיעִי לְשֵׁשֶׁת יְמֵי הַמַּעֲשֶׂה. בֵּין קְדֻשַּׁת שַׁבָּת לִקְדֻשַּׁת

Blessed are You, God, our God, King of the universe, who makes a distinction between sacred and profane, between light and darkness, between Israel and the nations, between the seventh day and the six workdays. You have made a distinction between

Kadesh

יוֹם טוֹב הִבְדַּלְתָּ, וְאֶת יוֹם הַשְּׁבִיעִי מִשֵּׁשֶׁת יְמֵי הַמַּעֲשֶׂה קִדַּשְׁתָּ. הִבְדַּלְתָּ וְקִדַּשְׁתָּ אֶת עַמְּךָ יִשְׂרָאֵל בִּקְדֻשָּׁתֶךָ. בָּרוּךְ אַתָּה יְיָ הַמַּבְדִּיל בֵּין קֹדֶשׁ לְקֹדֶשׁ.

the holiness of the *Shabbos* and the holiness of the festival, and You have sanctified the seventh day above the six workdays. You have set apart and made holy Your people Israel with Your holiness. Blessed are You, God, who makes a distinction between holy and holy.

Conclude with this brochah on the first night of Pesach:

בָּרוּךְ אַתָּה יְיָ אֱלֹהֵינוּ מֶלֶךְ הָעוֹלָם, שֶׁהֶחֱיָנוּ וְקִיְּמָנוּ וְהִגִּיעָנוּ לַזְּמַן הַזֶּה.

Blessed are You, God, our God, King of the universe, Who has granted us life, sustained us, and enabled us to reach this time.

"The Holy Spirit says: You [Pharaoh] say, 'In *case* they multiply,' but I say, '*Yes* will they multiply.' *Sotah* 11a

Urchatz

RITUAL WASHING IS not about removing *physical* dirt, but *spiritual* "dirt" called *tuma*. It is one thing to know the difference between holy and the profane, but a higher level of awareness to distinguish between the spiritually pure and impure, *tahor* and *tamei*.

Even the Jewish people require the Torah to define spiritual purity and impurity. Many of the underlying principles defy human logic and are *chukim*, or statutes, which, as *Rashi* explains, are the source of derision for skeptics.[1]

Becoming an "*Adam Shalaim*—Complete Person" means living with the reality of spiritual purity and impurity, and

---

[1] *Rashi, Bamidbar* 19:2.

Urchatz

trying to achieve the former. This is why the Talmud refers to the Jewish people as "*Adam*," and the gentile nations as the "*Umas HaOlam*—Nations of the World."[2]

Spiritual purity is a "system" for making sure that one is truly living a holy life, which is why there are so many laws of *tuma v'taharah* regarding the Temple and its service. Every Jew is supposed to be a temple in their own right so that God can dwell within them.[3] Even beyond the Temple a person has to try and maintain a higher level of spiritual purity.

The most severe level of *tuma* is a dead body. We were created to have a relationship with God, which a dead person cannot have, as it says, *"Neither will the dead praise God"* (*Tehillim* 115:17). *Tuma*, therefore represents a person's limitation to connect to God and must be removed to remove that limitation. Through this washing at the beginning of the *Seder*, we do this, if only symbolically.

Netilas Yadayim is also a reminder of Temple times when such a washing actually made a difference. Then a person had to be careful not to impart spiritual impurity to others or to food, which hands could do to wet food. Touching *karpas* dipped into salt water makes it susceptible to impurity from

---

[2] *Yevamos* 61a.
[3] *Shemos* 25:8.

Urchatz

our hands. Therefore, we first purify our hands, connecting us to Temple times and redemption.

The person leading the Seder washes their hands as if for bread except without the blessing, "al netilas yadayim." Some have the tradition of having the water brought to them at the table as royalty would.

---------- Something To Think About ----------

The exodus from Egypt liberated only *one out of five* Jews… Only those who desired redemption with all their hearts were redeemed. The Final Redemption likewise depends upon our yearning. *Ohr Yechezkel, Emunas HaGeulah,* p. 288

Karpas

THE WORD KARPAS in reverse is *Samech-Peh-Raish-Chof,* and alludes to the 600,000 Jews who suffered hard labor during Egyptian slavery. *Samech* equals 60, and the last three letters spell the word *parach*, which means "harsh." Therefore, the *karpas* is dipped into salt water because it represents the tears the Jewish people cried because of their slavery.

How does this part of the *Seder* help the growth process of the *Aleph* to make us an *Adam* and free? The essence of the growth process is *gilui Shechinah,* the revelation of the Divine Presence in the world, which is what the 10 plagues increasingly did. The more intellectually and emotionally tangible God's involvement in history becomes, the more powerful a soul becomes in everyday life.

The act of dipping *karpas* into salt water and eating it re-

Karpas

minds us about the impossible situation we, the Jewish people, once faced and how God overtly stepped into history to turn the tables on our oppressors and redeem us. It reminds us to not let adversity drain us of hope or make us assume that God doesn't care about us anymore. Not only will the difficult times end, but they will be followed by better times that can make us forget them.

But we shouldn't. Humility, the *Gemora* says, is one of the most important traits to develop and strengthen,[1] a major theme of the evening. It is the basis of self-honesty, which is central to become a *Tzelem Elokim*, someone acting in the "image of God." Recalling what it was like being down-and-out is always humbling.

Nothing stands in the way of *Aleph*-based growth more than *ga'avah*, unhealthy pride. As the Talmud says, Torah flows downward from Heaven, and only something lower can receive it.[2] Thus it says:

Moshe was very humble, more than anyone else… (*Bamidbar* 12:3)

This made Moshe *Rabbeinu* the fitting channel he was for God's Torah because it meant that he would not let personal

---

[1] *Avodah Zarah* 20b.
[2] *Eiruvin* 53b.

Karpas

bias distort his perception of truth. It is a way of telling us that the Torah Moshe gave over was the same version God told him. That's important for freedom because it says:

Rebi Yehoshua *ben* Levi said... "It says, *'The tablets were the work of God, and the writing was the writing of God, graven—charus—upon the tablets'* (*Shemos* 32:16). Don't read *charus*—graven, but *cheirus*—freedom, for there is no free person but one that occupies themself with the study of the Torah." (*Pirkei Avos* 6:2)

That is, the Torah God gave to us, not the one misinterpreted by those whose lack of humility prevents them from accurately passing on the word of God.

Everyone takes a vegetable (other than marror and often celery) and dips it into the salt water. **A piece smaller than a kezayis** *(less than 24 grams) should be used to avoid a doubtful after-blessing. The blessing is said with the marror in mind since it will also be eaten before the seudah.*

בָּרוּךְ אַתָּה יְיָ אֱלֹהֵינוּ מֶלֶךְ הָעוֹלָם, בּוֹרֵא פְּרִי הָאֲדָמָה.

Blessed are You, God, our God, King of the universe, Who creates fruit of the ground.

Yachatz

IT IS THE breaking of the middle *matzah* that transforms it into *Lechem Oni*—Poor Man's Bread. A poor person, not knowing if they'll have food tomorrow, rations what they have today.[1]

The *Maharal* goes deeper. He says that a *poor* person is actually a *free* person.[2] They are "free" to move at will because they are not tied down to any one place through any ownership of property. How many times throughout Jewish history have Jews lost their chance to escape danger because of their possessions? How many people might have already made *aliyah* if they weren't "stuck" paying off mortgages? It was one of the reasons why the 12,000,000 Jews died during the

---

[1] *Pesachim* 115b.
[2] *Haggadah Shel Pesach*.

Yachatz

Plague of Darkness.

Poor people tend to be humble people as well. Lacking status and worldly possessions, they have no way to compete with others, or to think more highly of themselves than they are. Humility is one of the most important traits and tools of a truth-seeker because subjective people distort truth for personal benefit.

Therefore, the *Mishnah* concludes:

This is the way of the Torah: Eat bread with salt, drink water in small measure, and sleep on the ground… (*Pirkei Avos* 6:4)

Does this mean that every Jew should divest themself of their wealth? This would suggest the opposite:

Four are considered as if they were dead: A pauper… (*Nedarim* 64b)

The resolution is summed up here:

At the time of the death of Rebi Yehudah *HaNasi*, he raised his ten fingers toward Heaven and said in prayer: "Master of the Universe, it is revealed and known before You that I toiled with my ten fingers in the Torah, and I have not derived any benefit from the world even with my small finger." (*Kesuvos* 104a)

Yachatz

That was quite a claim considering it says that *Rebi's* table never lacked anything, even during off seasons.[3] We can also assume that he dressed and acted the part of a prince of the Jewish people, who reportedly was close friends with Antonios.[4] What did *Rebi* mean?

He meant that he only took advantage of his material wealth and position as part of his service of God and on behalf of the Jewish people. He may have enjoyed the office and all of its perks, but it is not why he took or kept it. Though he personally benefited from what he had, he never had it for the sake of personal benefit. He did not define himself by material wealth, living the life of a rich man with the attitude of a poor one.

The Talmud adds:

There is no poor person except with respect to knowledge. (*Nedarim* 41a)

Perspective in life is everything. The right one makes a person happy and life meaningful, and the wrong one results in constant disappointment. But perspective is based upon perception, and perceptions are influenced by the assumptions we live with. Faulty assumptions mean faulty percep-

---

[3] *Avodah Zarah* 11a.
[4] *Avodah Zarah* 10b.

Yachatz

tions, and a faulty perspective on life.

Therefore, what a person knows makes the difference between true and mistaken ideas about freedom. No one will argue that having a lot of material possessions means a person is financially poor. But they will argue that being financially well off is not the key to ultimate freedom, and oftentimes hinders it. Poor Man's Bread warns us about this and encourages a person to think deeply about what truly makes them happy in life.

Matzah in general teaches this. *Chometz* represents bloated pride and is associated with the *yetzer hara,* a person's evil inclination.[5] But though we know how to avoid *chometz* in food, it is a lot harder to avoid it in life, unless a person takes the advice of this *mishnah* to heart:

If there is no flour, there is no Torah. (*Pirkei Avos* 3:21)

Obviously. But what is less obvious is this:

Flour comes from the grinding of wheat, which the Ultimate Wisdom made for this purpose. Through this man is distinguished from the animals, as already stated in the Talmud:

---

[5] The *yetzer hara* is called the *se'or sh'b'issa,* the leaven that is in the dough, because just as leaven "bloats" dough to make bread, the *yetzer hara* bloats a person's personality to make them believe they are more than they actually are (*Brochos* 17a).

Yachatz

When The Holy One, Blessed is He, told Adam, *"It will bring forth thorns and thistles"* (*Bereishis* 3:17), a tear formed in his eye. He said before Him, "Master of the Universe! Will I and my donkey eat from the same trough?!" (*Pesachim* 118a). Thus, had it not been that his food was ground finely, he would not have been able to achieve the completion of Torah (i.e., receive Torah at Mt. Sinai 26 generations later). (*Meiri, Pirkei Avos* 3:21)

The process of refining wheat into flour symbolizes the intellectual process of breaking down an idea to refine it, something an *Adam* must do to understand its essence and implications. The deeper a person probes, the more they expand their *Aleph* and the more *Adam* they become. The *matzah* hints to this as well.

This is why *Yachatz* also produces the *Afikomen*, which is hidden and then searched for by children at the *Seder*. We are training them to be truth-seekers, to use the Talmudic process throughout life to become a *chacham*—wise son, and avoid becoming an evil one. Ultimately, evil is the absence of good, something that is not always obvious from the outside.

The *Meiri* is explaining that had Adam *HaRishon* not realized he had intellectually descended to the level of a donkey, mankind would never have possessed the intellectual capaci-

Yachatz

ty to receive Torah at Mt. Sinai 26 generations later. We would have intellectually and spiritually stagnated, and *kemach*—flour—represents our transformation back in the direction of an *Adam*.

The problem happened again two millennia later when the Jewish people assimilated into Egyptian society, descending to the 49th level of spiritual impurity. This meant that they, effectively, "ate" from the same trough as the "donkey." The nine plagues helped to expand their *Aleph* and separate the Jewish people from the Egyptian people and, once again, flour in the form of *matzah* became the symbol.[6]

The *gematria* of *kemach*—flour—and *Pesach* are the same.[7] Replacing the word *kemach* with *Pesach* in the *mishnah* above, it reads: "if there is no *Pesach*, there is no Torah," that is *Shavuos,* the holiday that celebrates the receiving of Torah, 50 days after leaving Egypt.

The middle matzah is broken in two, and the smaller piece

---

[6] The *Maharal* explains that the Egyptian people, because of their obsession with material pleasures (*chomer*), were represented by the *chamor*, the donkey, which is also devoid of spirituality.

[7] *Kemach* is spelled with the letters, *Kuf* (100), *Mem* (40), and *Ches* (8), for 148. *Pesach* is spelled *Peh-Samech-Ches* (80+60+8), also totaling 148. According to *Kabbalah*, this makes the words interchangeable.

Yachatz

is placed back between the two other matzos. The larger piece is wrapped up as the Afikomen, and put over the shoulder as the fleeing Jews did in their time, and we say, "We leave Egypt in haste."

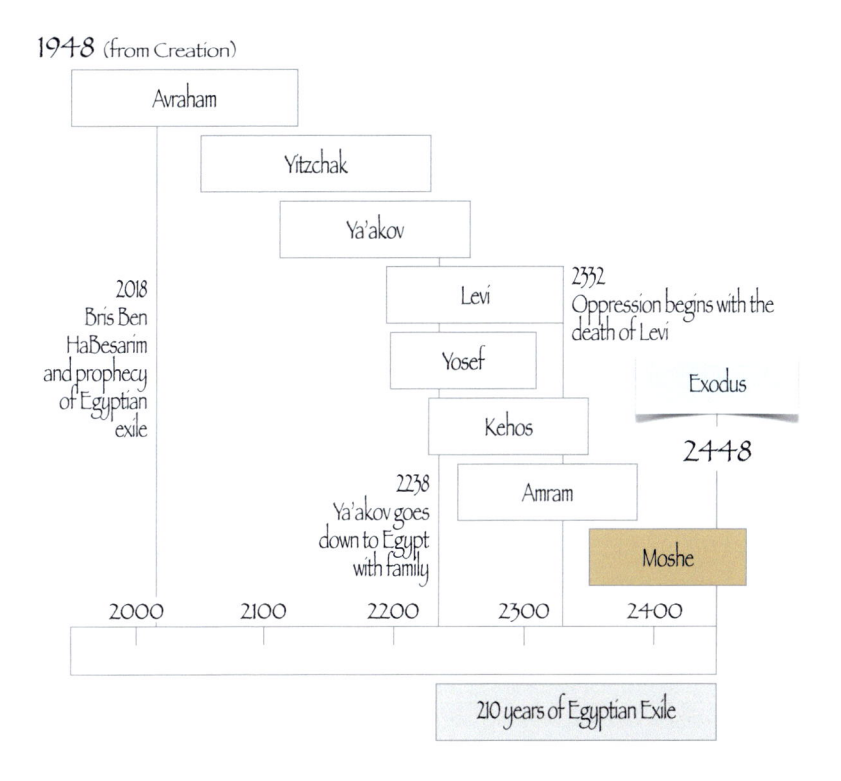

1948 (from Creation)

- Avraham
- Yitzchak
- Ya'akov
- Levi
- Yosef
- Kehos
- Amram
- Moshe

2018 Bris Ben HaBesarim and prophecy of Egyptian exile

2238 Ya'akov goes down to Egypt with family

2332 Oppression begins with the death of Levi

Exodus **2448**

2000 — 2100 — 2200 — 2300 — 2400

210 years of Egyptian Exile

35

Maggid

מַגִּיד

IMAGINE THE SURPRISE and excitement on everyone's face when I came out the first time dressed up as Moshe *Rabbeinu*, dramatizing the night of the first *Seder* in Egypt. I made sure to speak with a great sense of urgency, instructing everyone there as if they too were part of that initial redemption from Egypt.

After a few moments, the surprise transitioned to amusement. Adults laughed while children watched wide-eyed, taken in by the drama of the moment. My plan had worked better than any sweets could have, hooking the attention of all those at the *Seder* table. It made going through the rest of the story so much easier…for me as well. Nothing like an adrenalin rush to get your body into the moment.

My plan worked so well that dressing up and acting out the Exodus became family legend, and everyone looked forward

Maggid

to it each year after that. My challenge each *Seder* was to find a way to make it surprising and inspiring, even for those who knew what to expect. Eventually, I ordered a long, white wig and beard that allowed me to really look the part. Wrapping a broom handle in blue cellophane gave it a mystical sapphire look.

Eventually, we added a Pharaoh (my son) to the act, which added humor to the redemption drama. Then I would lead all those who would follow outside to miraculously cross an imaginary Red Sea, using my own sound effects to make it as real as possible. It was all quite tiring but also very exhilarating, and it has always provided us with momentum to get to the meal, no matter how late.

We make a *Seder* each year, not just to commemorate our redemption from Egyptian slavery, but to initiate and strengthen new generations, so that they can choose to carry on the message and the appreciation. The *Haggadah* provides the body of the *Seder*, but we have to put the soul into the evening if the tradition is to remain alive and vibrant for ourselves and our children.

It takes more than good learning habits to keep a three-millennia tradition alive. It takes inspiration, renewed each year by carrying out the *Pesach Seder* and recounting the story as if we too left Egypt.

Maggid

Lechem Oni (Poor Man's Bread) has three connotations: affliction (*inui*), poverty (*ani*), and answer (*oneh*). One, almost tasteless piece of unleavened bread reminds us of three things: our affliction in Egypt, the role of poverty in freedom, and that we should ask and answer many questions during the *Seder*.

The latter meaning is particularly relevant to *Maggid*, the "telling" of the story," and the questions and answers that follow. However, by this it should be clear that *matzah* itself is the answer. But what was the question?

The most obvious question is: Why do we exclusively eat *matzah* on *Pesach* as opposed to bread? The Torah answers this question with:

They could not delay, nor had they made provisions for themselves. (Shemos 12:39)

But why did they not have enough time to bake bread? How much time does it take to make *chometz*? Anyone who has seen *matzah* being baked knows that the problem is not too *little* time, but too *much* time. It is a frantic operation to make sure that the dough does not stay unworked for 18 minutes, at which time it becomes real *chometz*. No one had 18 minutes back in Egypt to let their dough rise while they made other preparations for the journey to freedom?

The traditional answer is that, being on the forty-ninth level

Maggid

of spiritual impurity that was Egyptian society, we had to avoid sinking to the fiftieth level at which point we could no longer be redeemed. By forcing Egypt to push the Jewish people out of Egypt, God saved us from spiritual oblivion and the *matzah* recalls that close call.

So *yes*, we eat *matzah* on *Pesach* because we did not have enough time to bake bread. But did we really have to leave Egypt so quickly to save the Jewish people? This says otherwise:

The commentators explain that they had to leave quickly in order to avoid descending to the fiftieth level of the Fifty Gates of Impurity. However, this does not seem to be correct, but just the opposite seems true! The strength of impurity had been eliminated as a result of the revelation of the Divine Presence [through each of the ten plagues], as it says, *"Not even a dog will growl for the Children of Israel"* (*Shemos* 11:7). He judged their gods and killed their firstborn, so how can it be that impurity had any control [at that point], *God forbid*? It is only relevant to say this at the end of the oppression and the beginning of the redemption [with the first. Had the redemption not begun [with the first plague[1]], and they had remained slaves in Egypt, then there would not

---

[1] After only 209 years of Egyptian exile, and not the 400 years God told Avraham about.

have been a rectification, *God forbid*, since they had entered the forty-ninth level of impurity…Once the redemption had already started however with the plagues twelve months the year before, the *Sitra Achra*[2] began to lose power and continued to do so from that time onward…By the month of *Nissan*, and especially on the first night of *Pesach*, it was completely beaten, conquered, and on the verge of destruction. Therefore, how could there have been any more concern about falling to the fiftieth gate [the night they made the *Seder*]? (*Drushei Olam HaTohu, Chelek* 2, *Drush* 5, *Anaf* 2 *Siman* 4)[3]

According to this, the Jewish people started to leave the Fifty Gates of Impurity with the first plague. When they sat down to make the first *Seder* in Egypt as God carried out the plague against the firstborn, the Jewish people were clear of *all* impurity:

It is impossible to say that the reason why they could not remain in Egypt was because they would fall to the fiftieth

---

[2] Literally, "Other Side," the name of the angel responsible for facilitating rebellion against God through sin. It is also called the "*Sattan*," which means "obstructor" because it interferes with people performing good.

[3] Rabbi Shlomo Elyashiv, *zt"l* (b. Šiauliai, Lithuania, 1841–d. Israel, 1926).

level, *God forbid*, since on the first night of *Pesach* impurity had no power at all. (*Drushei Olam HaTohu, Chelek* 2, *Drush* 5, *Anaf* 2 *Siman* 5)

Why then did they have to leave *b'chipazon*? For the opposite reason:

Since The Holy One, Blessed is He, emanated His holy light onto the Jewish people, as the author of the *Haggadah* writes, "The King of Kings was revealed to them" they could not remain in Egypt a moment longer or the *Sitra Achra* would have become completely eradicated, eliminating free-will, the purpose of Creation. (*Drushei Olam HaTohu, Chelek* 2, *Drush* 5, *Anaf* 2 *Siman* 5)

How radical. Firstly, we left quickly to save the *Egyptians*, not the *Jewish People*. Secondly, we had to save evil to save good.[4] What does all this mean, especially since the Talmud says:

In the time to come, The Holy One, Blessed is He, will bring the evil inclination and slay it in the presence of the right-

---

[4] The *Leshem* further explains: Egypt was the head of all [spiritual impurity at that time] and had it been destroyed then the *Sitra Achra* would also have been destroyed, as well as the *yetzer hara* (evil inclination). Free-will would no longer have existed, and for this reason they could not delay (*Drushei Olam HaTohu, Chelek* 2, *Drush* 5, *Anaf* 2, *Siman* 5).

eous and the wicked. (*Succah* 52a)

Why did God hold off on something that He plans to do later anyhow? Because:

Since this [redemption] was not the result of their own deeds, it was contrary to the purpose of Creation, and it was not possible for these wondrous lights[5] to remain since free-will would have ended…Therefore, the great light was removed from them immediately after the first night of *Pesach*, because it was intended that its continuation should be the result of their own deeds. (*Drushei Olam HaTohu, Chelek* 2, *Drush* 5, *Anaf* 2, *Siman* 5)

And we've been working on it ever since. Therefore, it says that…

One must look at themselves in each generation as if they too have come out of Egypt. (*Haggadah*)

…because each generation is just finishing what the previous ones did not, making the final redemption the last act of the first one.

This is why the final redemption is called *Keitz HaYomim*, literally "End of the Days." *The* days? *Which* days?[6] The days

---

[5] These were high spiritual lights that are not influenced by our deeds.
[6] It could just say, *Keitz Yomim*—End of Days.

that were left unfinished in Egypt because the Jewish people left 190 years early[7] to avoid becoming completely lost among the Egyptians. We've been completing those "days" now for over three millennia, and the final redemption will occur once that is complete. Therefore, the *gematria* of the word *keitz* is 190.[8]

The *matzah* does not so much symbolize what *was* accomplished, but what wasn't. Every year it is a reminder of our journey from Egypt, not the physical one but the spiritual one. *Sippur Yetzias Mitzrayim*, the recounting of the original physical departure from Egypt is supposed to further our ongoing spiritual departure from *Mitzrayim*.

Though Egypt is a physical reality, *Mitzrayim* is a conceptual one, one that is not tied to any one geographical location. Any nation can become, because of its value system, the *Mitzrayim* of its time. The Jewish people left Egypt with Moshe, but we've been leaving *Mitzrayim* ever since.

The name itself *Mitzrayim* indicates this. It is spelled, *Mem-Tzaddi-Raish-Yud-Mem* which, according to *Kabbalah*, is two Hebrew words: *meitzer* (*Mem-Tzaddi-Raish*), which

---

[7] The prophecy was for 400 years (*Bereishis* 15:13), but we left after only 210 years to avoid falling to the fiftieth level of spiritual impurity.
[8] *Ben Ish Chai*.

means *boundary*, and *yum* (*Yud-Mem*), which means *sea*.⁹ But *Yud-Mem* also has a *gematria* of ten plus forty, which totals fifty, an allusion to the Fifty Gates of Understanding with which the world was created:

Fifty Gates of Understanding were created in the world, and all of them were given to Moshe except for one. (*Rosh Hashanah* 21b)

Mitzrayim therefore is *any* culture that stifles the Fifty Gates of Understanding, which are the basis of Torah. Leaving *Mitzrayim* conceptually means overcoming such intellectual and spiritual obstacles, something that will only happen if:

If you want it like money and seek it like buried treasures, then you will understand fear of God, and Godly knowledge you will find. (Mishlei 2:4-5)

Hence, the *Afikomen*. That is the piece of the middle *matzah* hidden for children to seek as a "buried treasure," to bring home the wisdom of Shlomo *HaMelech's* words.

Raise the broken matzah for everyone to see and say:

הָא לַחְמָא עַנְיָא דִי אֲכָלוּ אַבְהָתָנָא בְּאַרְעָא דְמִצְרָיִם.

This is the bread of affliction that our fathers ate in the land

---

⁹ *Drushei Olam HaTohu, Chelek* 2, *Drush* 5, *Anaf* 4, *Siman* 3.

Maggid

כָּל דִכְפִין יֵיתֵי וְיֵיכֹל, כָּל דִצְרִיךְ יֵיתֵי וְיִפְסַח. הָשַׁתָּא הָכָא, לְשָׁנָה הַבָּאָה בְּאַרְעָא דְיִשְׂרָאֵל. הָשַׁתָּא עַבְדֵי, לְשָׁנָה הַבָּאָה בְּנֵי חוֹרִין.

of Egypt. All who are hungry, let them come and eat. All who need, let them come and make the *Pesach* Offering. This year we are here. Next year, in *Eretz Yisroel*. This year we are slaves. Next year, free people.

ESSENTIALLY THIS IS a *mitzvah* of *tzedakah*. The *Brisker Rav* explains its inclusion here as a kind of right of passage. The analogy is of a young prince who leaves the palace to live among the commoners, only to realize after time that he misses the palace. By that time however the king, his father, has forsaken him, especially since he no longer looks like a prince. But the noble who pleads on the prince's behalf before the king points out the similarity between the king's face and that of his son. This arouses the king's mercy, and he accepts his son back into the palace.

Likewise, the Jewish people caused themselves to be exiled among the nations of the world, and after time began to look and behave like the people of their host nations. Eventually their Father in Heaven, the King of Kings, ceased to recognize them, even as they sit down to make a *Pesach Seder*.

But one of the main characteristics of the Jewish people is

their charitable nature, through which we become recognizable to God once again. Therefore, having begun *Maggid* with an act of *tzedakah*, we can now proceed with the *Seder* knowing that God has one again recognized us as His people.

The Four Questions

THE FOUR QUESTIONS set the tone, not just for the *Seder* but for life in general. As one person put it: "Some parents bronze their child's first pair of shoes. A Jewish parent 'bronzes' their child's first *kasha*—strong question."

This is because a *kasha* shows that the child is paying attention to life, that they are sensitive to *nuances of difference* that often lead to profound insights. It is too easy for a person to take life for granted, and when they do, they miss out on personal growth and so much hidden opportunity to accomplish.

Everything that man has invented was usually an answer to a question or challenge someone had. The smartest and most capable people in society tend to be the ones who pay attention to the world around them, and then ask the best questions about it, which the *Haggadah* is encouraging from a young age.

Maggid

Remove the Seder plate from the table, pour the second cup of wine, and ask the following questions. It is enough for one child to ask all the questions, but many families encourage all the children to showcase how well they learned "Di Fir Kashes" (The Four Questions). It is also one of the best opportunities to involve the children before they fall asleep.

מַה נִּשְׁתַּנָּה הַלַּיְלָה הַזֶּה מִכָּל הַלֵּילוֹת?

What makes this night different from all [other] nights?

שֶׁבְּכָל הַלֵּילוֹת אָנוּ אוֹכְלִין חָמֵץ וּמַצָּה, הַלַּיְלָה הַזֶּה כֻּלּוֹ מַצָּה!

On all nights we eat *chometz* or *matzah*, and on this night only *matzah*.

שֶׁבְּכָל הַלֵּילוֹת אָנוּ אוֹכְלִין שְׁאָר יְרָקוֹת, הַלַּיְלָה הַזֶּה מָרוֹר!

On all nights we eat any kind of vegetables, and on this night *marror*!

שֶׁבְּכָל הַלֵּילוֹת אֵין אָנוּ מַטְבִּילִין אֲפִילוּ פַּעַם אֶחָת, הַלַּיְלָה הַזֶּה שְׁתֵּי פְעָמִים!

On all nights we need not dip even once, on this night we do so twice!

שֶׁבְּכָל הַלֵּילוֹת אָנוּ אוֹכְלִין בֵּין יוֹשְׁבִין וּבֵין מְסֻבִּין, הַלַּיְלָה הַזֶּה כֻּלָּנוּ מְסֻבִּין!

On all nights we eat sitting upright or reclining, and on this night we all recline!

It never gets old, though it really could. The same questions and the same answers each year? But that's the point, they're neither the same questions nor the same answers, though the words never change. But we do, and life does as well, and therefore, so does a person's perspective on life. A "different" person with a different perspective makes the same questions different each year.

Curious children often grow up to become smart adults. The right kind of curiosity at the right time leads to great discoveries and can often *save* lives. So many of the important insights in life have been found by people who paid attention enough to ask the subtle questions and find their profound answers.

Amalek, the Biblical nemesis of the Jewish people,[10] constantly uses distraction and spiritual desensitization to enslave minds. It doesn't matter what their means is, but if it is something that casts doubt on the existence of God and the relevance of Torah, it is Amalekian. This is why "Amalek," in *gematria*, is equal to the *gematria* of "*suffek*—doubt."[11] We

---

[10] *Shemos* 17:8. The nation of Amalek is long gone, but their mentality and alarming approach to truth will remain until the Messianic Era.
[11] Amalek is *Ayin-Mem-Lamed-Kuf,* which equals 70+40+30+100, which equals 240. *Suffek* is *Samech-Peh-Kuf*, which equals 60+80+100, or 240.

fight doubt, Amalek, intellectual enslavement—and eventually physical enslavement—when we do the opposite.

Thus it says:

The Tablets are the handiwork of God, and the writing was God's writing *charus*—engraved—on the Tablets. Don't read "*charus*," but "*cheirus*"—freedom—because there is no freer person than one who engages in Torah study. (*Pirkei Avos* 6:2)

It is a convenient play on words,[12] but many have begged to differ over three millennia. Torah is *mitzvos*, 613 to be exact, and there are countless details to keep in mind to do them right. It takes time and a lot of self-discipline to live a Torah life, and that seems very confining from the "outside"…to a person who is uninterested in reaching their personal level of *Aleph*.

Human perfection is not automatic or easy. Just like wheat must be planted, nurtured, harvested, ground, and then sifted to make edible food, and perhaps even seasoned, likewise a human has to be developed to bring out their *Aleph* and lead them to personal freedom. That is the goal of Torah.

Quite simply, *mitzvos* spiritually refine a person. They are

---

[12] *Charus* and *cheirus* have the same Hebrew letters, just different vowels.

not just a disciplined way of life, which all societies acknowledge is necessary, but a *Divinely*-disciplined way of life. By following the direction of Torah, the soul of a person is able to channel the body's energy in an ultimately meaningful way. *Mitzvos* "feed" the *Aleph*, make it stronger, and provide life:

"For the living know that they will die" (*Koheles* 9:5): these are the righteous who in death are called "living"..."*But the dead know nothing*" (*Shmuel* 2:23:20): these are the wicked who during their lifetime are called "dead." (*Brochos* 18a)

This is how we fulfill the following:

Choose life that you may live, you and your seed, to love God your God, to listen to His voice and to cling to Him. That is your life and length of your days, so that you may dwell in the land which God swore to your fathers...to give them. (*Devarim* 30:19-20)

There are *four* sons, *four* questions, and *four* cups of wine because the number *four* alludes to another prominent message of the *Seder* and freedom process. Even the prophesied 400 years of exile and the 40 years of desert wandering are multiples of four. The soul of a fetus enters the body after 40 days from conception.[13]

---

[13] *Brochos* 60a.

Maggid

The number four, which corresponds to the Hebrew letter *Dalet*, emphasizes the importance of humility in achieving freedom. *Dalet* is spelled *Dalet-Lamed-Tav*, the first two letters spelling the word *dal*—poor person, who is usually a *humble* person. This is how Moshe *Rabbeinu* found the Jewish people at the beginning of the exodus from Egypt, broken and completely humbled:

Moshe spoke to the Children of Israel, but they did not listen to Moshe because of [their] shortness of breath and [their] hard labor. (Shemos 6:9)

Return the Seder plate. Reveal the matzos during the telling of the story.

עֲבָדִים הָיִינוּ לְפַרְעֹה בְּמִצְרָיִם וַיּוֹצִיאֵנוּ יְיָ אֱלֹהֵינוּ מִשָּׁם בְּיָד חֲזָקָה וּבִזְרוֹעַ נְטוּיָה. וְאִלּוּ לֹא הוֹצִיא הַקָּדוֹשׁ בָּרוּךְ הוּא אֶת אֲבוֹתֵינוּ מִמִּצְרַיִם, הֲרֵי אָנוּ וּבָנֵינוּ וּבְנֵי בָנֵינוּ מְשֻׁעְבָּדִים הָיִינוּ לְפַרְעֹה בְּמִצְרָיִם. וַאֲפִילוּ כֻּלָּנוּ חֲכָמִים, כֻּלָּנוּ נְבוֹנִים, כֻּלָּנוּ זְקֵנִים, כֻּלָּנוּ יוֹדְעִים אֶת

We were slaves to Pharaoh in Egypt, and God, our God, took us out from there with a strong hand and with an outstretched arm. If The Holy One, Blessed is He, had not taken our fathers out of Egypt, then we, our children and our children's children would have remained slaves to Pharaoh in Egypt. Even if all of us were wise, all of us understanding,

Maggid

הַתּוֹרָה, מִצְוָה עָלֵינוּ לְסַפֵּר בִּיצִיאַת מִצְרָיִם. וְכָל הַמַּרְבֶּה לְסַפֵּר בִּיצִיאַת מִצְרַיִם הֲרֵי זֶה מְשֻׁבָּח.

all of us knowing the Torah, we would still be obligated to discuss the exodus from Egypt. Everyone who discusses the exodus from Egypt at length is praiseworthy.

How is this the answer to the questions? Because it was our humble beginning, the turning point at which we went from *gannai*—disgrace—as the *Gemora* calls it,[14] to honorable redemption. It is said that "those who forget are doomed to repeat." To make sure we don't repeat, we make sure not to forget. Therefore, even if all of us are wise, of understanding, and knowing of Torah, we tell the story each year…

מַעֲשֶׂה בְּרַבִּי אֱלִיעֶזֶר וְרַבִּי יְהוֹשֻׁעַ וְרַבִּי אֶלְעָזָר בֶּן עֲזַרְיָה, וְרַבִּי עֲקִיבָא וְרַבִּי טַרְפוֹן, שֶׁהָיוּ מְסֻבִּין בִּבְנֵי בְרַק, וְהָיוּ מְסַפְּרִים בִּיצִיאַת מִצְרַיִם כָּל אוֹתוֹ הַלַּיְלָה, עַד שֶׁבָּאוּ תַלְמִידֵיהֶם וְאָמְרוּ לָהֶם:

Once, Rebi Eliezer, Rebi Yehoshua, Rebi Elazar *ben* Azariah, Rebi Akiva and Rebi Tarphon were reclining in Bnei Brak. They were discussing the exodus from Egypt all that night, until their students came and told

---

[14] *Pesachim* 116a.

Maggid

"רַבּוֹתֵינוּ, הִגִּיעַ זְמַן קְרִיאַת שְׁמַע שֶׁל שַׁחֲרִית!" them: *"Our Masters! The time has come for reciting the morning Shema!"*

In one paragraph we are told what it means to truly recount the story of leaving Egypt. A person is where their heart is, and if it is not in the same place as their mind then the task will be laborious and tiring. There will always seem like *too* much time, unlike what occurred for these rabbis. They were *physically* in Bnei Brak thirteen centuries after the *Yetzias Mitzrayim*, but their hearts and minds were in Egypt back at the time of the exodus, so they lost track of the current time. For these rabbis, the story went from being just a story to life itself.

אָמַר אֶלְעָזָר בֶּן עֲזַרְיָה: "הֲרֵי אֲנִי כְּבֶן שִׁבְעִים שָׁנָה, וְלֹא זָכִיתִי שֶׁתֵּאָמֵר יְצִיאַת מִצְרַיִם בַּלֵּילוֹת, עַד שֶׁדְּרָשָׁהּ בֶּן זוֹמָא: שֶׁנֶּאֱמַר "לְמַעַן תִּזְכֹּר אֶת יוֹם צֵאתְךָ מֵאֶרֶץ מִצְרַיִם, כֹּל יְמֵי חַיֶּיךָ" (דברים טז:ג): "יְמֵי חַיֶּיךָ"...הַיָּמִים, "כֹּל יְמֵי חַיֶּיךָ"...הַלֵּילוֹת. וַחֲכָמִים Rebi Elazar *ben* Azariah said: "I am like a 70-year old man, yet I could not prove that the exodus from Egypt must be mentioned at night until Ben Zoma explained it. It says *'That you may remember the day you left Egypt all the days of your life'* (*Devarim* 16:3). Now, *'the days of your life'* refers to the days, [and the additional word]

53

Maggid

אוֹמְרִים: "יְמֵי חַיֶּיךָ"...הָעוֹלָם הַזֶּה, "כֹּל יְמֵי חַיֶּיךָ"...לְהָבִיא לִימוֹת הַמָּשִׁיחַ.

'all' indicates the nights as well!" The rabbis said: "'*The days of your life*' refers to the present world; *'all'* includes the days of *Moshiach*."

He was only *like* a 70-year old man because he was actually only 17 years old when he assumed the leadership of the Jewish people. But to add to his credibility (everyone else around him was the older and wiser age they looked), a miracle happened, and Rebi Elazar's hair turned white like a man three times his age. The question is, what does *any* of this have to do with *Sippur Yetzias Mitzrayim*, the recounting of the story of the exodus?

Just as the number four is connected to the theme of redemption, so is the number seventy. *Kabbalistically*, seventy is the amount of spiritual lights that must emanate down into our world for redemption to occur. Thus, redemption from Bavel and the story of Purim occurred no less than seventy years after the exile began.

Seventy is also the number of wisdom:

One who becomes "settled" through wine has the *da'as*—knowledge—of their Creator...has the *da'as*—knowledge of the *seventy* Elders. Wine was given with *seventy* letters, and the secret was given with *seventy* letters. When wine goes in, secrets go out. (*Eiruvin* 65a)

The numerical value of wine in Hebrew is seventy (*Yud-Yud-Nun*), as is the word *sod* (*Samech-Vav-Dalet*), which is why they are equated. But what does this have to do with becoming "settled" through wine and having Godly knowledge?

Wine is unique because of its balance of fruitiness, acidity, bitterness, and body, which makes it such a subtle-yet-captivating beverage. But unlike grape juice, wine is also intoxicating, and this affects the body, not the soul. In a sense, wine neutralizes the body, allowing the soul more freedom. That is the "*sod*" that is supposed to emerge when wine goes in.

The Talmud says that prior to birth a fetus is taught the entire Torah, which they are made to forget at birth.[15] But why give all that knowledge if only to take it away before it can be used?

Because it is easier to recall something that was forgotten than to learn something completely new. There is a pre-existing relationship to the knowledge that education recovers, which explains that sense of familiarity we have when we learn something for the "first" time. This means that education is really just the process of bringing knowledge from the

---
[15] *Niddah* 30b.

subconscious mind to the conscious one.

Why don't we just know all that knowledge automatically? Because the body is so distracted by the outside world that it blocks it. Education becomes easier when the body gets out of the way, which is why the best teachers seem to be good "entertainers" as well. Wine helps with this if the body is only neutralized so the soul can come out, but not if the opposite results.

In this sense, wine reveals the true nature of a person as well. This is what the Talmud means when it says:

Rebi Elai said: In three ways a person's true character is revealed: his *kos*—cup, his *keese*—wallet, and in his *ka'as*—anger. (*Eiruvin* 65b)

The connection of all this to the mentioning of the leaving of Egypt at nighttime as well as daytime? Nighttime is compared to exile, and the leaving of Egypt was redemption, which is compared to daytime. Why speak about redemption (daytime) during a time of exile (nighttime)?

Because that is the best way to start leaving it. Even though we think we are free people because we live in open societies, we begin the *Seder* by declaring, "This year [we are] slaves…next year [we will be] free people." This indicates that we are still in exile as long the *Shechinah* is in exile, and that won't change until the Third Temple is built and all the

Jewish people have returned to *Eretz Yisroel*.

It is still the night of exile, and yet we celebrate the redemption from Egypt. But the *Seder* and *matzah* only celebrate our departure from the first *Mitzrayim*, not all of those which have followed. So they also remind us of the redemption yet to come, and the work we have to do to make the final one a reality.

Like *Drush*, which reveals the hidden, inner meaning of a Torah idea, for which Ben Zoma was known, we use wine, which represents *Da'as*—Godly knowledge—to bring out our "secret," our hidden, inner soul. To do this is to experience *Yetzias Mitzrayim* on a personal level.

The Four Sons

WE'VE DISCUSSED THE significance of the number four, the role of good education in Torah transmission, and the underlying intent of the Evil Son's question (Introduction). Many others have discussed the four sons in detail, their questions and the answers to them. But what is also important to know is how all four sons are in each one of us at times.

Everyone at times has acted like the *Chacham* (Wise Son), letting truth matter more than personal biases, or like the *Rasha* (Evil Son) by doing the opposite. We have all been a

Maggid

Tam (Simple Son) when confronted by a truth so new that we do know what to make of it, or like someone who can't ask a question because we are too naive about something to even ask one.

Similarly, there are times when we embrace Torah and want to understand it, and times when we reject some aspect of it for some reason. Sometimes we just go with the flow, while other times we question in detail. We have to recognize this and how to deal with it so that we can reach the level with which we are about to start: "Blessed is The Place, *blessed is He*! Blessed is He Who gave the Torah to His people Israel, *blessed is He!*"

בָּרוּךְ הַמָּקוֹם, בָּרוּךְ הוּא. בָּרוּךְ שֶׁנָּתַן תּוֹרָה לְעַמּוֹ יִשְׂרָאֵל, בָּרוּךְ הוּא.

Blessed is The Place, *blessed is He*! Blessed is He Who gave the Torah to His people Israel, *blessed is He!*

There are many names for God, each of which refers to a different *aspect* of God's revelation to man, never His Essence. God's Essence is beyond understanding and therefore, description. The name of God used here, *HaMakom*—The Place—is one of the less common ones, especially in this context.

The Name means that God is the *place* of all existence.[16] His light is not only in every aspect of Creation, but all of Creation exists within Him. There is no place that God is not, because the moment He withdraws His light from something it doesn't just die; it ceases to exist at all. To know this in one's mind *and* heart is to achieve the ultimate God consciousness. It is to become as real with life as humanly possible and a *chacham* in the full sense of the word, the goal of life.

So we thank "The Place" for giving us Torah, without which we could not do any of this. After millennia of history and billions of people, most still grope in the dark for the purpose of life, even concluding that there really isn't one. The four "sons" are the product of different approaches for this ultimate truth.

כְּנֶגֶד אַרְבָּעָה בָנִים דִּבְּרָה תּוֹרָה: אֶחָד חָכָם, וְאֶחָד רָשָׁע, וְאֶחָד תָּם, וְאֶחָד שֶׁאֵינוֹ יוֹדֵעַ לִשְׁאוֹל.

Correspondingly, the Torah speaks of four sons, one wise, one evil, one who is simple, and one who does not know how to ask a question.

חָכָם מָה הוּא אוֹמֵר? "מַה הָעֵדוֹת וְהַחֻקִּים וְהַמִּשְׁפָּטִים

What does the wise one say? "What are the testimonies, the

---

[16] *Nefesh HaChaim, Sha'ar 3.*

Maggid

אֲשֶׁר צִוָּה יְיָ אֱלֹהֵינוּ אֶתְכֶם?" וְאַף אַתָּה אֱמָר לוֹ כְּהִלְכוֹת הַפֶּסַח: "אֵין מַפְטִירִין אַחַר הַפֶּסַח אֲפִיקוֹמָן."

רָשָׁע מָה הוּא אוֹמֵר? "מָה הָעֲבֹדָה הַזֹּאת לָכֶם?" (שמות יב:כו), לָכֶם, וְלֹא לוֹ. וּלְפִי שֶׁהוֹצִיא אֶת עַצְמוֹ מִן הַכְּלָל, כָּפַר בְּעִקָּר. וְאַף אַתָּה הַקְהֵה אֶת שִׁנָּיו וֶאֱמָר לוֹ: "בַּעֲבוּר זֶה עָשָׂה יְיָ לִי בְּצֵאתִי מִמִּצְרָיִם" (שמות יג:ח), לִי, וְלֹא לוֹ. אִילוּ הָיָה שָׁם, לֹא הָיָה נִגְאָל.

תָּם מָה הוּא אוֹמֵר? "מַה זֹּאת? וְאָמַרְתָּ אֵלָיו: בְּחֹזֶק יָד הוֹצִיאָנוּ יְיָ מִמִּצְרַיִם, מִבֵּית עֲבָדִים" (שמות יג: יד).

statutes, and the laws which God, our God, has commanded you?" Tell him about the laws of the Pesach Offering, [up to] "one is not allowed to eat anything after the *Afikomen*."

What does the evil one say? *"What is this service to you?!"* "To you," but not to him! By excluding himself from the nation he denies fundamentals.

Therefore blunt his teeth and tell him: *"It is because of this that God did [what He did] for me when I left Egypt."* "For me," but not for him! Had he been there, he would not have been redeemed!

What does the simple one say? "What is this?" Tell him: *"With a strong hand God took us out of Egypt, from the house of slaves."*

Maggid

וְשֶׁאֵינוֹ יוֹדֵעַ לִשְׁאוֹל אַתְּ פְּתַח לוֹ, שֶׁנֶּאֱמַר: "וְהִגַּדְתָּ לְבִנְךָ בַּיּוֹם הַהוּא לֵאמֹר: בַּעֲבוּר זֶה עָשָׂה יְיָ לִי בְּצֵאתִי מִמִּצְרָיִם" (שמות יג:ח).

For the one who does not know how to even ask [a question], begin for him and say: *"Tell your child on that day: It is because of this that God did [what He did] for me when I left Egypt."*

יָכוֹל מֵרֹאשׁ חֹדֶשׁ? תַּלְמוּד לוֹמַר "בַּיּוֹם הַהוּא." אִי "בַּיּוֹם הַהוּא" יָכוֹל מִבְּעוֹד יוֹם? תַּלְמוּד לוֹמַר "בַּעֲבוּר זֶה": בַּעֲבוּר זֶה לֹא אָמַרְתִּי, אֶלָּא בְּשָׁעָה שֶׁיֵּשׁ מַצָּה וּמָרוֹר מֻנָּחִים לְפָנֶיךָ.

One might think that [the telling] should be from the first of the month. The Torah therefore says, *"On that day."* If "on that day," you might think while it is still day. The Torah says, *"because of this."* It says "because of this" [to say], only when *matzah* and *marror* are placed before you.

What's the first *mitzvah* the Jewish people received? *Rosh Chodesh*, the *mitzvah* to sanctify the new moon.[17] We re-

---

[17] *Shemos* 12:1.

ceived it before even leaving Egypt, which might seem strange since it was a *mitzvah* that we could not actually do until we conquered and settled *Eretz Yisroel*.

But more than other *mitzvos, Kiddush HaChodesh,* the *mitzvah* to sanctify the new moon, is emblematic of why the Jewish people were miraculously taken out of Egypt in the first place. The moon, as luminous as it can be in the night sky has no source of light of its own. It only reflects the light of the sun to the earth.

Similarly, the Jewish people, represented by the moon, as "bright" as they might be, are here to reflect the light of God —the light of Torah—to mankind. Therefore, does that not make *Rosh Chodesh* the ideal time to recount the Exodus? One might have thought so, so the Torah tells us otherwise, while the *Haggadah* brings up the idea to remind us of the reason God stepped into history and miraculously redeemed His people.

And so we begin to recount the story, but not in the middle of it with the Exodus itself, but at the *actual* beginning. Even going down to Egypt as "seventy souls" in Yosef's time was already late. This is the *true* beginning of how the Jewish people went from being only a concept to an actual nation of God.

Maggid

מִתְּחִלָּה עוֹבְדֵי עֲבוֹדָה זָרָה הָיוּ אֲבוֹתֵינוּ, וְעַכְשָׁיו קֵרְבָנוּ הַמָּקוֹם לַעֲבֹדָתוֹ, שֶׁנֶּאֱמַר: וַיֹּאמֶר יְהוֹשֻׁעַ אֶל כָּל הָעָם: "כֹּה אָמַר יְהוָה אֱלֹהֵי יִשְׂרָאֵל: בְּעֵבֶר הַנָּהָר יָשְׁבוּ אֲבוֹתֵיכֶם מֵעוֹלָם, תֶּרַח אֲבִי אַבְרָהָם וַאֲבִי נָחוֹר, וַיַּעַבְדוּ אֱלֹהִים אֲחֵרִים. וָאֶקַּח אֶת אֲבִיכֶם, אֶת אַבְרָהָם, מֵעֵבֶר הַנָּהָר וָאוֹלֵךְ אוֹתוֹ בְּכָל אֶרֶץ כְּנַעַן, וָאַרְבֶּה אֶת זַרְעוֹ וָאֶתֶּן לוֹ אֶת יִצְחָק. וָאֶתֵּן לְיִצְחָק אֶת יַעֲקֹב וְאֶת עֵשָׂו, וָאֶתֵּן לְעֵשָׂו אֶת הַר שֵׂעִיר לָרֶשֶׁת אוֹתוֹ, וְיַעֲקֹב וּבָנָיו יָרְדוּ מִצְרָיִם" (יהושע כד:ב).

בָּרוּךְ שׁוֹמֵר הַבְטָחָתוֹ לְיִשְׂרָאֵל, בָּרוּךְ הוּא. שֶׁהַקָּדוֹשׁ בָּרוּךְ הוּא חִשַּׁב אֶת הַקֵּץ, לַעֲשׂוֹת כְּמוֹ שֶׁאָמַר לְאַבְרָהָם אָבִינוּ

In the beginning our fathers served idols, but now God has brought us close to His service, as it says: *"Yehoshua said to all the people: 'So says God, God of Israel, "Your fathers used to live on the other side of the river, Terach, the father of Avraham and the father of Nachor, and they served other gods. I took your father Avraham from beyond the river, and I led him throughout the whole land of Canaan. I increased his seed and gave him Yitzchak, and to Yitzchak I gave Ya'akov and Eisav. To Eisav I gave Mt. Seir to possess it, and Ya'akov and his sons went down to Egypt."*

Blessed is He who keeps His promise to Israel, blessed be He! For the Holy One, Blessed is He, calculated the end [of the slavery], in order to do as He had said to our father

Maggid

בִּבְרִית בֵּין הַבְּתָרִים, שֶׁנֶּאֱמַר: וַיֹּאמֶר לְאַבְרָם: "יָדֹעַ תֵּדַע כִּי גֵר יִהְיֶה זַרְעֲךָ בְּאֶרֶץ לֹא לָהֶם, וַעֲבָדוּם, וְעִנּוּ אֹתָם אַרְבַּע מֵאוֹת שָׁנָה. אֶת הַגּוֹי אֲשֶׁר יַעֲבֹדוּ דָּן אָנֹכִי, וְאַחֲרֵי כֵן יֵצְאוּ בִּרְכֻשׁ גָּדוֹל. (בראשית טו:יד)

Avraham at the "Pact of the Halves," as it says: "And He said to Avraham, *'Know your children will be strangers in a land that is not theirs, and they will enslave them and make them suffer, for 400 years. But I shall also judge the nation whom they serve, and after that they will go out with great wealth.'"*

Cover the matzos and raise the cup of wine.

וְהִיא שֶׁעָמְדָה לַאֲבוֹתֵינוּ וְלָנוּ, שֶׁלֹּא אֶחָד בִּלְבָד עָמַד עָלֵינוּ לְכַלּוֹתֵנוּ, אֶלָּא שֶׁבְּכָל דּוֹר וָדוֹר עוֹמְדִים עָלֵינוּ לְכַלּוֹתֵנוּ, וְהַקָּדוֹשׁ בָּרוּךְ הוּא מַצִּילֵנוּ מִיָּדָם.

This is what has stood by our fathers and us! For not just one alone has risen against us to destroy us, but they rise against us in every generation to destroy us, but The Holy One, Blessed is He, saves us from their hand!

Uncover the matzos and put down the cup of wine.

צֵא וּלְמַד מַה בִּקֵּשׁ לָבָן

Go and learn what Lavan the

Maggid

הָאֲרַמִּי לַעֲשׂוֹת לְיַעֲקֹב אָבִינוּ. שֶׁפַּרְעֹה לֹא גָזַר אֶלָּא עַל הַזְּכָרִים וְלָבָן בִּקֵּשׁ לַעֲקוֹר אֶת הַכֹּל, שֶׁנֶּאֱמַר: **אֲרַמִּי אֹבֵד אָבִי, וַיֵּרֶד מִצְרַיְמָה, וַיָּגָר שָׁם בִּמְתֵי מְעָט, וַיְהִי שָׁם לְגוֹי גָּדוֹל עָצוּם וָרָב.** (דברים כו: ה)

Aramean wanted to do to our father Ya'akov. Pharaoh had issued a decree against the male children only, but Lavan wanted to uproot everyone, as it says: *"The Aramean wanted to destroy my father, and he went down to Egypt and sojourned there, few in number, and he became there a nation, great and mighty and numerous."*

Some have pointed out the historical impossibility of Jewish survival, given all the conditions the nation has had to persevere over millennia. Exile, assimilation, intermarriage and, above all, terrible anti-Semitism and persecution, statistically-speaking, should have put an end to the Jewish people long ago. Not only have they survived, they have even thrived, pointing to some kind of *supernatural* resistance to complete destruction.

וַיֵּרֶד מִצְרַיְמָה...אָנוּס עַל פִּי הַדִּבּוּר. **And he went down to Egypt**...they were forced [to go down] by God.

Maggid

And he sojourned there... this teaches that Ya'akov *Avinu* did not go down to Egypt to settle, but only to live there temporarily, as it says, *"They said to Pharaoh, 'We have come to sojourn in the land, for there is no pasture for the flocks of your servants because the hunger is severe in Canaan. Please let your servants live in the land of Goshen.'"*

וַיָּגָר שָׁם...מְלַמֵּד שֶׁלֹּא יָרַד יַעֲקֹב אָבִינוּ לְהִשְׁתַּקֵּעַ בְּמִצְרַיִם אֶלָּא לָגוּר שָׁם, שֶׁנֶּאֱמַר: "וַיֹּאמְרוּ אֶל פַּרְעֹה, לָגוּר בָּאָרֶץ בָּאנוּ, כִּי אֵין מִרְעֶה לַצֹּאן אֲשֶׁר לַעֲבָדֶיךָ, כִּי כָבֵד הָרָעָב בְּאֶרֶץ כְּנָעַן, וְעַתָּה יֵשְׁבוּ נָא עֲבָדֶיךָ בְּאֶרֶץ גֹּשֶׁן" (בראשית מז:ד).

It has been the reason for so much disaster, staying too long in one place of exile or another. The moment Ya'akov *Avinu* saw that Lavan and his sons were less friendly to him,[18] he took it has a Divine sign to return home. He didn't just brace himself and hope that the anti-Semitism would get better and not worse, as countless Jewish communities have done, and *do*, ever since with tragically disastrous results.

One of the themes of the *Haggadah* is a message to Jews throughout the ages: You're not home until you are actually

---

[18] *Bereishis* 31:2.

Maggid

home in *Eretz Yisroel*. Exiles come to an end, and surviving them often depends upon knowing when to leave the one you're currently living through.

בִּמְתֵי מְעָט...כְּמָה שֶׁנֶּאֱמַר: "בְּשִׁבְעִים נֶפֶשׁ יָרְדוּ אֲבֹתֶיךָ מִצְרָיְמָה, וְעַתָּה שָׂמְךָ יְיָ אֱלֹהֶיךָ כְּכוֹכְבֵי הַשָּׁמַיִם לָרֹב" (דברים י:כב).

Few in number...As it says: *"Your fathers went down to Egypt with seventy people, and now, God, your God, has made you as numerous as the stars of heaven."*

וַיְהִי שָׁם לְגוֹי...מְלַמֵּד שֶׁהָיוּ יִשְׂרָאֵל מְצֻיָּנִים שָׁם.

And he became a nation there...this teaches that Israel was distinctive there.

גָּדוֹל עָצוּם...כְּמוֹ שֶׁנֶּאֱמַר: "וּבְנֵי יִשְׂרָאֵל פָּרוּ וַיִּשְׁרְצוּ וַיִּרְבּוּ וַיַּעַצְמוּ בִּמְאֹד מְאֹד, וַתִּמָּלֵא הָאָרֶץ אֹתָם" (שמות א:ז).

Great, mighty...As it says: *"And the Children of Israel were fruitful and greatly increased, and multiplied and became very, very mighty, and the land became filled with them."*

וָרָב...כְּמָה שֶׁנֶּאֱמַר: רְבָבָה כְּצֶמַח הַשָּׂדֶה נְתַתִּיךְ, וַתִּרְבִּי וַתִּגְדְּלִי וַתָּבֹאִי בַּעֲדִי עֲדָיִים, שָׁדַיִם נָכֹנוּ וּשְׂעָרֵךְ צִמֵּחַ וְאַתְּ עֵרֹם וְעֶרְיָה. וָאֶעֱבֹר עָלַיִךְ

And numerous...As it says: *"I made you as numerous as the plants of the field; you grew and developed, and became charming and beautiful*

Maggid

וָאֶרְאֵךְ מִתְבּוֹסֶסֶת בְּדָמָיִךְ, וָאֹמַר לָךְ: בְּדָמַיִךְ חֲיִי, וָאֹמַר לָךְ: בְּדָמַיִךְ חֲיִי. (יחזקאל טז:ו)

וַיָּרֵעוּ אֹתָנוּ הַמִּצְרִים וַיְעַנּוּנוּ, וַיִּתְּנוּ עָלֵינוּ עֲבֹדָה קָשָׁה. (דברים כו:ו)

וַיָּרֵעוּ אֹתָנוּ הַמִּצְרִים...כְּמָה שֶׁנֶּאֱמַר: "הָבָה נִתְחַכְּמָה לוֹ פֶּן יִרְבֶּה, וְהָיָה כִּי תִקְרֶאנָה מִלְחָמָה וְנוֹסַף גַּם הוּא עַל שֹׂנְאֵינוּ וְנִלְחַם בָּנוּ וְעָלָה מִן הָאָרֶץ" (שמות א:י).

וַיְעַנּוּנוּ...כְּמָה שֶׁנֶּאֱמַר: "וַיָּשִׂימוּ עָלָיו שָׂרֵי מִסִּים לְמַעַן עַנֹּתוֹ בְּסִבְלֹתָם. וַיִּבֶן עָרֵי מִסְכְּנוֹת לְפַרְעֹה, אֶת פִּתֹם וְאֶת רַעַמְסֵס" (שמות א:יא).

of form, with hair grown long. But you were naked and bare, and I passed over you and saw you wallowing in your blood, and I said to you 'By your blood you will live,' and I said to you 'By your blood you will live!'"

The Egyptians treated us badly and they made us suffer, and they put hard work upon us.

The Egyptians treated us badly...as it says: *"Come, let us act wisely with him in case they multiply and, if there should be a war against us, they will join our enemies, fight against us and leave the land."*

And they made us suffer...as it says: *"They put taskmasters over them to make them suffer with their burdens, and they built storage cities for Pharaoh, Pisom and Ramses."*

Maggid

וַיִּתְּנוּ עָלֵינוּ עֲבֹדָה קָשָׁה... כְּמָה שֶׁנֶּאֱמַר: "וַיַּעֲבִדוּ מִצְרַיִם אֶת בְּנֵי יִשְׂרָאֵל בְּפָרֶךְ" (שמות א:יג).

וַנִּצְעַק אֶל יהוה אֱלֹהֵי אֲבֹתֵינוּ, וַיִּשְׁמַע יהוה אֶת קֹלֵנוּ, וַיַּרְא אֶת עָנְיֵנוּ וְאֶת עֲמָלֵנוּ וְאֶת לַחֲצֵנוּ. (דברים כו:ז)

וַנִּצְעַק אֶל יְיָ אֱלֹהֵי אֲבֹתֵינוּ... כְּמָה שֶׁנֶּאֱמַר: "וַיְהִי בַיָּמִים הָרַבִּים הָהֵם וַיָּמָת מֶלֶךְ מִצְרַיִם, וַיֵּאָנְחוּ בְנֵי יִשְׂרָאֵל מִן הָעֲבוֹדָה וַיִּזְעָקוּ, וַתַּעַל שַׁוְעָתָם אֶל הָאֱלֹהִים מִן הָעֲבֹדָה" (שמות ב:כג).

וַיִּשְׁמַע יְיָ אֶת קֹלֵנוּ... כְּמָה שֶׁנֶּאֱמַר: "וַיִּשְׁמַע אֱלֹהִים אֶת נַאֲקָתָם, וַיִּזְכֹּר אֱלֹהִים אֶת בְּרִיתוֹ אֶת אַבְרָהָם, אֶת יִצְחָק וְאֶת יַעֲקֹב" (שמות ב:כד).

And they put hard work upon us...as it says, *"The Egyptians made the Children of Israel work with rigor."*

And we cried out to God, the God of our fathers, and God heard our voice and saw our suffering, our labor and our oppression.

And we cried out to the God, God of our fathers... as it says: *"During that long period, the king of Egypt died; and the Children of Israel groaned because of the servitude, and they cried out. And their cry for help from their servitude rose up to God."*

And God heard our voice...as it says: *"And God heard their groaning, and God remembered His covenant with Avraham, Yitzchak and Ya'akov."*

Maggid

וַיַּרְא אֶת עָנְיֵנוּ...זוֹ פְּרִישׁוּת דֶּרֶךְ אֶרֶץ, כְּמָה שֶׁנֶּאֱמַר: "וַיַּרְא אֱלֹהִים אֶת בְּנֵי יִשְׂרָאֵל וַיֵּדַע אֱלֹהִים" (שמות ב:כה).

And he saw our suffering...this refers to the separation of husband and wife, as it is said: *"God saw the Children of Israel and God knew."*

וְאֶת עֲמָלֵנוּ...אֵלּוּ הַבָּנִים, כְּמָה שֶׁנֶּאֱמַר: "כָּל הַבֵּן הַיִּלּוֹד הַיְאֹרָה תַּשְׁלִיכֻהוּ וְכָל הַבַּת תְּחַיּוּן" (שמות א:כב).

Our labor...this refers to the children, as it says: *"Every boy that is born, you shall throw into the river and every girl you shall keep alive."*

וְאֶת לַחֲצֵנוּ...זוֹ הַדְּחַק, כְּמָה שֶׁנֶּאֱמַר: "וְגַם רָאִיתִי אֶת הַלַּחַץ אֲשֶׁר מִצְרַיִם לֹחֲצִים אֹתָם" (שמות ג:ט).

And our oppression...this refers to the pressure, as it says: *"I have seen the oppression with which the Egyptians oppress them."*

All of this, of course, is the backstory of *Yetzias Mitzrayim*. But do we read it just for the sake of continuity, or is there a deeper message? There's *always* a deeper message, in this case about the way to look at Jewish history.

Human beings are limited in what they know and how they find out about things. They also cannot control everything, so many things can happen without their knowledge, or not according to their plan. People they care about can suffer for a while before they find out about it to "save" them.

Not God, though. It can certainly look like that, but it is not the reality. Not only does God know all things at all times… not only does He have complete control over everything that happens…but He is the One *making* it happen, *when* it happens, *as* it happens. As disconnected as the redemption may seem from the exile, it is not at all.

That may not bring solutions to problems any earlier. But there is something comforting and encouraging in knowing that the struggles are not random or meaningless, but actually part of the redemption process. They have been Divinely calibrated to accomplish specific things at different stages to make redemption possible. We have to believe that, and trust God for the process.

וַיּוֹצִאֵנוּ יְהוָה מִמִּצְרַיִם בְּיָד חֲזָקָה וּבִזְרֹעַ נְטוּיָה וּבְמֹרָא גָּדֹל, וּבְאֹתוֹת וּבְמֹפְתִים. (דברים כו:ח)	*God took us out of Egypt with a strong hand and an outstretched arm, and with a great awe, and with signs and wonders.*
וַיּוֹצִאֵנוּ יְיָ מִמִּצְרַיִם…לֹא עַל יְדֵי מַלְאָךְ, וְלֹא עַל יְדֵי שָׂרָף, וְלֹא עַל יְדֵי שָׁלִיחַ, אֶלָּא הַקָּדוֹשׁ בָּרוּךְ הוּא בִּכְבוֹדוֹ וּבְעַצְמוֹ, שֶׁנֶּאֱמַר: **"וְעָבַרְתִּי**	**God took us out of Egypt**… not through an angel, not through a *seraph* and not through a messenger. The Holy One, blessed be He, did it in His glory by Himself, as it

Maggid

בְּאֶרֶץ מִצְרַיִם בַּלַּיְלָה הַזֶּה, וְהִכֵּיתִי כָל בְּכוֹר בְּאֶרֶץ מִצְרַיִם מֵאָדָם וְעַד בְּהֵמָה, וּבְכָל אֱלֹהֵי מִצְרַיִם אֶעֱשֶׂה שְׁפָטִים, אֲנִי יְיָ" (שמות יב:יב).

וְעָבַרְתִּי בְאֶרֶץ מִצְרַיִם **בַּלַּיְלָה הַזֶּה**...אֲנִי וְלֹא מַלְאָךְ.

וְהִכֵּיתִי כָל בְכוֹר בְּאֶרֶץ **מִצְרַיִם**...אֲנִי וְלֹא שָׂרָף.

וּבְכָל אֱלֹהֵי מִצְרַיִם אֶעֱשֶׂה **שְׁפָטִים**...אֲנִי וְלֹא הַשָּׁלִיחַ.

אֲנִי יְיָ...אֲנִי הוּא וְלֹא אַחֵר.

בְּיָד חֲזָקָה...זוֹ הַדֶּבֶר, כְּמָה שֶׁנֶּאֱמַר: "הִנֵּה יַד יְיָ הוֹיָה בְּמִקְנְךָ אֲשֶׁר בַּשָּׂדֶה: בַּסּוּסִים, בַּחֲמֹרִים, בַּגְּמַלִּים, בַּבָּקָר וּבַצֹּאן, דֶּבֶר כָּבֵד מְאֹד" (שמות ט:ג).

says: *"In that night I will pass through the land of Egypt, and I will kill every firstborn in the land of Egypt, from man to animal, and I will carry out judgments against all the gods of Egypt, I, God."*

I will pass through the land of Egypt...I and not an angel.

And I will smite every firstborn in the land of Egypt...I and not a seraph;

And I will carry out judgments against all the gods of Egypt...I and not a messenger;

I, God...It is I, and none other!

With a strong hand...This refers to the disease, as it is said: *"Behold, the hand of God will be upon your livestock in the field, upon the horses, the*

Maggid

וּבִזְרֹעַ נְטוּיָה...זוֹ הַחֶרֶב, כְּמָה שֶׁנֶּאֱמַר: "וְחַרְבּוֹ שְׁלוּפָה בְּיָדוֹ, נְטוּיָה עַל יְרוּשָׁלָיִם" (דברי הימים א כא:טז).

וּבְמֹרָא גָּדֹל...זוֹ גִּלּוּי שְׁכִינָה, כְּמָה שֶׁנֶּאֱמַר: "אוֹ הֲנִסָּה אֱלֹהִים לָבוֹא לָקַחַת לוֹ גוֹי מִקֶּרֶב גּוֹי, בְּמַסֹּת בְּאֹתֹת וּבְמוֹפְתִים וּבְמִלְחָמָה וּבְיָד חֲזָקָה וּבִזְרוֹעַ נְטוּיָה וּבְמוֹרָאִים גְּדֹלִים, כְּכֹל אֲשֶׁר עָשָׂה לָכֶם יְהוָה אֱלֹהֵיכֶם בְּמִצְרַיִם לְעֵינֶיךָ" (דברים ד:לד).

וּבְאֹתוֹת...זֶה הַמַּטֶּה, כְּמָה שֶׁנֶּאֱמַר: "וְאֶת הַמַּטֶּה הַזֶּה תִּקַּח בְּיָדְךָ, אֲשֶׁר תַּעֲשֶׂה בּוֹ אֶת הָאֹתֹת" (שמות ד:יז).

donkeys, the camels, the herds and the flocks, a very severe disease."

And with an outstretched arm...This refers to the sword, as it says: *"His sword was drawn, in his hand, stretched out over Jerusalem."*

And with a great awe...This refers to the revelation of the Divine Presence, as it says: *"Has any God ever tried to take for Himself a nation from within another nation, with trials, signs and wonders, with war and with a strong hand and an outstretched arm, and with a great awe, like all that God your God, did for you in Egypt before your eyes!"*

And with signs...This refers to the staff, as it is said: *"Take into your hand this staff with which you shall perform the signs."*

Maggid

וּבְמֹפְתִים...זֶה הַדָּם, כְּמָה שֶׁנֶּאֱמַר: "וְנָתַתִּי מוֹפְתִים בַּשָּׁמַיִם וּבָאָרֶץ..." **And wonders**...this refers to the blood, as it says: *"And I shall show wonders in heaven and on earth..."*

When saying the words, "blood, fire, and pillars of smoke," spill three times from the wine in the cup. Do not remove wine by dipping a finger, but by spilling from the cup itself, and do so into a broken/chipped dish.

"דָּם וָאֵשׁ וְתִימְרוֹת עָשָׁן"... (יואל ג:ג). *...Blood, and fire, and pillars of smoke."*

Why spend so much time elucidating these verses? By this point in the *Seder*, many are anxious to get to the meal, especially since it is late, the children are tired, and people are hungry. There is a tendency by now to "just want to get through it."

What we're really doing is showing God how much we appreciate what He did for us, and still does. If someone thanks you for your help in general terms, it means they don't fully appreciate your kindness. But if they enumerate different parts of your *chesed*, it means they not only noticed each aspect but that they are grateful for each one as well.

Maggid

The *yetzer hara* is lazy in this respect, and it doesn't appreciate how important *hakoras hatov*—recognition of the good—is to God, and happiness. The more blessed a person feels, the happier they are…the *freer* they are. And all they have to do is take note of what they already have but take for granted, usually because they've had it for so long already.

But for every blessing a person has, there are people without it. Even if a person feels miserable, there are people who feel worse, missing things that they have. Counting one's blessings is not just good advice. It is the secret to peace of mind.

More importantly, it is the secret to a close relationship with the "Source of all Blessing," God. Showing Him how much we *sincerely* appreciate every last detail of His kindnesses to us is the best way to ensure that they keep coming.

דָּבָר אַחֵר: בְּיָד חֲזָקָה... שְׁתַּיִם, וּבִזְרֹעַ נְטוּיָה... שְׁתַּיִם, וּבְמֹרָא גָּדֹל... שְׁתַּיִם, וּבְאֹתוֹת... שְׁתַּיִם, וּבְמֹפְתִים... שְׁתַּיִם. אֵלוּ עֶשֶׂר מַכּוֹת שֶׁהֵבִיא הַקָּדוֹשׁ בָּרוּךְ הוּא עַל הַמִּצְרִים בְּמִצְרַיִם, וְאֵלּוּ הֵן:

Another explanation is: "Strong hand" [refers to] two [plagues], "outstretched arm" [to] two, "great awe" [to] two, "signs" [to] two, and "wonders" [to] two [plagues]. These are the Ten Plagues which the Holy One, Blessed is He, brought upon the Egyptians, and they are:

Maggid

דָּם, צְפַרְדֵּעַ, כִּנִּים, עָרוֹב, דֶּבֶר, שְׁחִין, בָּרָד, אַרְבֶּה, חֹשֶׁךְ, מַכַּת בְּכוֹרוֹת.

Blood. Frogs. Lice. Wild Beasts. Pestilence. Boils. Hail. Locust. Darkness. Death of the First-born.

When saying the ten plagues, spill from the cup itself ten times.

רַבִּי יְהוּדָה הָיָה נוֹתֵן בָּהֶם סִמָּנִים: דְּצַ"ךְ עֲדַ"שׁ בְּאַחַ"ב.

Rebi Yehudah used acronyms: *DeTzaCh, ADaSh, BeAChaV.*

רַבִּי יוֹסֵי הַגְּלִילִי אוֹמֵר: מִנַּיִן אַתָּה אוֹמֵר שֶׁלָּקוּ הַמִּצְרִים בְּמִצְרַיִם עֶשֶׂר מַכּוֹת, וְעַל הַיָּם לָקוּ חֲמִשִּׁים מַכּוֹת? בְּמִצְרַיִם מָה הוּא אוֹמֵר? "וַיֹּאמְרוּ הַחַרְטֻמִּים אֶל פַּרְעֹה: 'אֶצְבַּע אֱלֹהִים הִוא'" (שמות ח:טו). וְעַל הַיָּם מָה הוּא אוֹמֵר? "וַיַּרְא יִשְׂרָאֵל אֶת הַיָּד הַגְּדֹלָה אֲשֶׁר עָשָׂה יְיָ בְּמִצְרַיִם, וַיִּירְאוּ הָעָם אֶת יְיָ, וַיַּאֲמִינוּ בַּיְיָ וּבְמֹשֶׁה עַבְדּוֹ."

Rebi Yosi *HaGallili* said: "How do we know that the Egyptians were stricken by ten plagues in Egypt, and then were struck by fifty plagues at the sea? In Egypt it says, *'The magicians said to Pharaoh, 'This is the finger of God.'* At the sea it says, *'Israel saw the great hand that God used against Egypt; and the people feared God, and they believed in God and in His servant Moshe.'* Now, how often were they afflicted by [the] 'finger' [of God]? Ten plagues! Thus, in Egypt they

Maggid

(שמות יד:לא). כַּמָּה לָקוּ בָאֶצְבַּע? עֶשֶׂר מַכּוֹת אֱמוֹר מֵעַתָּה: בְּמִצְרַיִם לָקוּ עֶשֶׂר מַכּוֹת וְעַל הַיָּם לָקוּ חֲמִשִּׁים מַכּוֹת.

רַבִּי אֱלִיעֶזֶר אוֹמֵר: מִנַּיִן שֶׁכָּל מַכָּה וּמַכָּה שֶׁהֵבִיא הַקָּדוֹשׁ בָּרוּךְ הוּא עַל הַמִּצְרִים בְּמִצְרַיִם הָיְתָה שֶׁל אַרְבַּע מַכּוֹת? שֶׁנֶּאֱמַר: "יְשַׁלַּח בָּם חֲרוֹן אַפּוֹ, עֶבְרָה וָזַעַם וְצָרָה, מִשְׁלַחַת מַלְאֲכֵי רָעִים" (תהלים עח:מט). עֶבְרָה... אַחַת, וָזַעַם...שְׁתַּיִם, וְצָרָה.... שָׁלֹשׁ, מִשְׁלַחַת מַלְאֲכֵי רָעִים...אַרְבַּע. אֱמוֹר מֵעַתָּה: בְּמִצְרַיִם לָקוּ אַרְבָּעִים מַכּוֹת וְעַל הַיָּם לָקוּ מָאתַיִם מַכּוֹת.

רַבִּי עֲקִיבָא אוֹמֵר: מִנַּיִן שֶׁכָּל מַכָּה וּמַכָּה שֶׁהֵבִיא הַקָּדוֹשׁ בָּרוּךְ הוּא עַל

were afflicted by ten plagues, and at the sea they were afflicted by fifty plagues!"

Rebi Eliezer said: "How do we know that each individual plague which The Holy One, Blessed is He, brought upon the Egyptians in Egypt consisted of four plagues? Because it says: *'He sent against them His fierce anger, fury, and indignation, and trouble, a discharge of messengers of evil'*— 'fury,' is one; 'indignation,' is two; 'trouble,' is three, and 'discharge of messengers of evil,' makes four. Therefore, now say that in Egypt they were afflicted by forty plagues, and at the sea they were afflicted by two hundred plagues."

Rebi Akiva said: "How do we know that each individual plague which The Holy One, Blessed is He, brought upon the Egyptians in Egypt consist-

Maggid

הַמִּצְרִים בְּמִצְרַיִם הָיְתָה שֶׁל חָמֵשׁ מַכּוֹת? שֶׁנֶּאֱמַר: "יְשַׁלַּח בָּם חֲרוֹן אַפּוֹ, עֶבְרָה וָזַעַם וְצָרָה, מִשְׁלַחַת מַלְאֲכֵי רָעִים". חֲרוֹן אַפּוֹ...אַחַת, עֶבְרָה...שְׁתַּיִם, וָזַעַם...שָׁלֹשׁ, וְצָרָה...אַרְבַּע, מִשְׁלַחַת מַלְאֲכֵי רָעִים...חָמֵשׁ. אֱמֹר מֵעַתָּה: בְּמִצְרַיִם לָקוּ חֲמִשִּׁים מַכּוֹת וְעַל הַיָּם לָקוּ חֲמִשִּׁים וּמָאתַיִם מַכּוֹת.

ed of five plagues? It says: *'He sent against them His fierce anger, fury, and indignation, and trouble, a discharge of messengers of evil.'* 'His fierce anger' is one, 'fury' is two, 'indignation,' is three, 'trouble,' is four, and 'discharge of messengers of evil' makes five. Now you have to say that in Egypt they were afflicted by fifty plagues, and at the sea they were afflicted by two hundred and fifty plagues."

Every miracle can be seen as a collection of smaller miracles. For example, birth is a great miracle, but there are countless "smaller" miracles that have to first happen before the general miracle of birth can occur. Should any of the smaller ones not occur, then something can go tragically wrong with the birth itself, or later in life.

Thanks to technology, we can now see so many more of those "smaller" miracles previously invisible to us, not just regarding birth, but with respect to so many other aspects of life. It certainly helps to enhance a person's sense of awe, and most important of all, their appreciation of everything about this world. As mentioned earlier, appreciation is the name of this game we call "Life."

No one would question that being able to feel gratitude is an important part of being human. What many may not realize though is that it is the basis of our most important, *Godly* trait: humility. It is *humbling* to realize how much of life is a gift, a function of the soul.

Entitlement, on the other hand, usually originates from the body and tends to compel a person to act selfishly. It has been said that "happiness begins where selfishness ends," and that a happy person is a freer one. By appreciating all the many miracles that make life and accomplishment possible, selflessness results and with it, personal freedom.

These rabbis showed us how. Now we'll do it as well.

How many levels of favors God did for us! **כַּמָה מַעֲלוֹת טוֹבוֹת לַמָּקוֹם עָלֵינוּ!**

If He had brought us out of Egypt and not judged them, *it would have been enough for us!*

אִלּוּ הוֹצִיאָנוּ מִמִּצְרַיִם וְלֹא עָשָׂה בָּהֶם שְׁפָטִים, דַּיֵּינוּ.

If He had judged them and not their gods, *it would have been enough for us!*

אִלּוּ עָשָׂה בָּהֶם שְׁפָטִים, וְלֹא עָשָׂה בֵאלֹהֵיהֶם, דַּיֵּינוּ.

Maggid

אִלּוּ עָשָׂה בֵאלֹהֵיהֶם, וְלֹא הָרַג אֶת בְּכוֹרֵיהֶם, דַּיֵּנוּ.	If He had judged their gods, and had not killed their firstborn, *it would have been enough for us!*
אִלּוּ הָרַג אֶת בְּכוֹרֵיהֶם, וְלֹא נָתַן לָנוּ אֶת מָמוֹנָם, דַּיֵּנוּ.	If He had killed their firstborn, and had not given us their wealth, *it would have been enough for us!*
אִלּוּ נָתַן לָנוּ אֶת מָמוֹנָם, וְלֹא קָרַע לָנוּ אֶת הַיָּם, דַּיֵּנוּ.	If He had given us their wealth, and had not split the sea for us, *it would have been enough for us!*
אִלּוּ קָרַע לָנוּ אֶת הַיָּם, וְלֹא הֶעֱבִירָנוּ בְּתוֹכוֹ בֶּחָרָבָה, דַּיֵּנוּ.	If He had split the sea for us, and had not taken us through it on dry land, *it would have been enough for us!*
אִלּוּ הֶעֱבִירָנוּ בְּתוֹכוֹ בֶּחָרָבָה, וְלֹא שִׁקַּע צָרֵנוּ בְּתוֹכוֹ, דַּיֵּנוּ.	If He had taken us through the sea on dry land, and had not drowned our oppressors in it, *it would have been enough for us!*
אִלּוּ שִׁקַּע צָרֵנוּ בְּתוֹכוֹ, וְלֹא סִפֵּק צָרְכֵּנוּ בַּמִּדְבָּר אַרְבָּעִים שָׁנָה, דַּיֵּנוּ.	If He had drowned our oppressors in it, and had not supplied our needs in the desert for forty years, *it would*
אִלּוּ סִפֵּק צָרְכֵּנוּ בַּמִּדְבָּר אַרְבָּעִים שָׁנָה, וְלֹא הֶאֱכִילָנוּ אֶת הַמָּן, דַּיֵּנוּ.	
אִלּוּ הֶאֱכִילָנוּ אֶת הַמָּן, וְלֹא נָתַן לָנוּ אֶת הַשַּׁבָּת, דַּיֵּנוּ.	

Maggid

אִלּוּ נָתַן לָנוּ אֶת הַשַּׁבָּת, וְלֹא קֵרְבָנוּ לִפְנֵי הַר סִינַי, דַּיֵּינוּ.

אִלּוּ קֵרְבָנוּ לִפְנֵי הַר סִינַי, וְלֹא נָתַן לָנוּ אֶת הַתּוֹרָה, דַּיֵּינוּ.

אִלּוּ נָתַן לָנוּ אֶת הַתּוֹרָה, וְלֹא הִכְנִיסָנוּ לְאֶרֶץ יִשְׂרָאֵל, דַּיֵּינוּ.

אִלּוּ הִכְנִיסָנוּ לְאֶרֶץ יִשְׂרָאֵל, וְלֹא בָנָה לָנוּ אֶת בֵּית הַבְּחִירָה, דַּיֵּינוּ.

have been enough for us!

If He had supplied our needs in the desert for forty years, and had not fed us *mann*, it would have been enough for us!

If He had fed us *mann*, and had not given us *Shabbos*, it would have been enough for us!

If He had given us *Shabbos*, and had not brought us to Mt. Sinai, *it would have been enough for us!*

If He had brought us to Mt. Sinai, and had not given us the Torah, *it would have been enough for us!*

If He had given us the Torah, and had not brought us into *Eretz Yisroel, it would have been enough for us!*

If He had brought us into *Eretz Yisroel*, and had not built the Temple, *it would have been enough for us!*

עַל אַחַת כַּמָּה וְכַמָּה, טוֹבָה כְפוּלָה וּמְכֻפֶּלֶת לַמָּקוֹם

How much more so should we be grateful to God for the doubled and redoubled good-

Maggid

עָלֵינוּ: שֶׁהוֹצִיאָנוּ מִמִּצְרַיִם, וְעָשָׂה בָהֶם שְׁפָטִים, וְעָשָׂה בֵאלֹהֵיהֶם, וְהָרַג אֶת בְּכוֹרֵיהֶם, וְנָתַן לָנוּ אֶת מָמוֹנָם, וְקָרַע לָנוּ אֶת הַיָּם, וְהֶעֱבִירָנוּ בְּתוֹכוֹ בֶּחָרָבָה, וְשִׁקַּע צָרֵנוּ בְּתוֹכוֹ, וְסִפֵּק צָרְכֵּנוּ בַּמִּדְבָּר אַרְבָּעִים שָׁנָה, וְהֶאֱכִילָנוּ אֶת הַמָּן, וְנָתַן לָנוּ אֶת הַשַּׁבָּת, וְקֵרְבָנוּ לִפְנֵי הַר סִינַי, וְנָתַן לָנוּ אֶת הַתּוֹרָה, וְהִכְנִיסָנוּ לְאֶרֶץ יִשְׂרָאֵל, וּבָנָה לָנוּ אֶת בֵּית הַבְּחִירָה לְכַפֵּר עַל כָּל עֲוֹנוֹתֵינוּ.

ness that He has done for us. He has brought us out of Egypt, carried out judgments against them and against their gods, killed their firstborn, gave us their wealth, split the sea for us, took us through it on dry land, drowned our oppressors in it, supplied our needs in the desert for forty years, fed us the *mann*, gave us *Shabbos*, brought us to Mt. Sinai, gave us the Torah, brought us to *Eretz Yisroel*, and built the Temple for us to atone for all our sins.

Really? It would have been enough to just have left Egypt, or to have inherited Egyptian wealth, or to arrive at Mt. Sinai but not receive Torah? Actually, *no*. The entire point of the redemption from Egypt was to get to Mt. Sinai and receive the Torah. Had we not, the Talmud explains, the world would have returned back to the null and void of Creation![19]

The answer is, the world around us. Billions of people for

---

[19] *Shabbos* 88a.

millennia have been okay with basic levels of existence. Everyday people get up in the morning and go to bed at night having done little more than survive the day. All that counts for many is getting to the end of life with as few struggles as possible and some pleasure along the way.

We acknowledge here that we might have been like that also, had God not taken us the full spiritual distance. Like most others, we would have been satisfied just to survive and enjoy whatever we could get from life. It would have been "enough" though, as we found out, there is so much more.

But after seeing what that "more" looks like, we can now be eternally grateful for it. The opportunity for personal fulfillment is so much greater, and life is so much more profound. Only after receiving all of it can we appreciate what life would have been like without it.[20]

Once, a *ba'al teshuvah* at the beginning of his return to Torah told God, "You owe me! I could have easily been happy living a secular life, but I sacrificed all of that for You and Your Torah. So, I think you owe Me for that!"

After learning Torah for another year, he came to realize how much more meaningful his life was because he "happened" to discover the Torah way of life. At that point he revised his

---

[20] See the *Radak, Hoshea* 3:2 who says something similar.

previous claim and told God, "Maybe it's more 50-50. You helped me discover truth, and I sacrificed to live it."

After another year of learning he realized that, had he *not* discovered Torah, he would have missed out on the greatest opportunity of his life. In the end, he gave up nothing, but was just very fortunate that God had the patience to wait for his return. Now he told God, "I'm so sorry it took me so long to return home. I owe *You* everything!"

We have grown up with expressions like, "What you don't know won't hurt you" and, "A little bit of knowledge is a dangerous thing." When it comes to appreciating what God has done for us, they can never be true. And it's our level of gratitude that so greatly enhances our joy in life.

רַבָּן גַּמְלִיאֵל הָיָה אוֹמֵר: כָּל שֶׁלֹּא אָמַר שְׁלֹשָׁה דְבָרִים אֵלּוּ בַּפֶּסַח, לֹא יָצָא יְדֵי חוֹבָתוֹ, וְאֵלּוּ הֵן: Rabban Gamliel used to say: "Whoever does not discuss the following three things on *Pesach* has not fulfilled their obligation, and they are:

פֶּסַח, מַצָּה, וּמָרוֹר. *Pesach, Matzah, and Marror.*

Point at the shank bone (or similar), but do not pick it up, and say:

Maggid

פֶּסַח שֶׁהָיוּ אֲבוֹתֵינוּ אוֹכְלִים בִּזְמַן שֶׁבֵּית הַמִּקְדָּשׁ הָיָה קַיָּם, עַל שׁוּם מָה?

עַל שׁוּם שֶׁפָּסַח הַקָּדוֹשׁ בָּרוּךְ הוּא עַל בָּתֵּי אֲבוֹתֵינוּ בְּמִצְרַיִם, שֶׁנֶּאֱמַר: "וַאֲמַרְתֶּם זֶבַח פֶּסַח הוּא לַה', אֲשֶׁר פָּסַח עַל בָּתֵּי בְנֵי יִשְׂרָאֵל בְּמִצְרַיִם בְּנָגְפּוֹ אֶת מִצְרַיִם, וְאֶת בָּתֵּינוּ הִצִּיל, וַיִּקֹּד הָעָם וַיִּשְׁתַּחֲווּ" (שמות יב:כז).

Pesach, which our fathers ate during the time of the Temple, was for which reason?

Because God passed over our ancestors' houses in Egypt, as it says: *"You shall say, It is a Pesach to God, because He passed over the houses of the Children of Israel in Egypt when He struck the Egyptians with a plague, and He saved our houses. And the people bowed and prostrated themselves."*

Lift the broken matzah and say:

מַצָּה זוֹ שֶׁאָנוּ אוֹכְלִים, עַל שׁוּם מָה? עַל שׁוּם שֶׁלֹּא הִסְפִּיק בְּצֵקָם שֶׁל אֲבוֹתֵינוּ לְהַחֲמִיץ, עַד שֶׁנִּגְלָה עֲלֵיהֶם מֶלֶךְ מַלְכֵי הַמְּלָכִים הַקָּדוֹשׁ בָּרוּךְ הוּא וּגְאָלָם, שֶׁנֶּאֱמַר: "וַיֹּאפוּ אֶת הַבָּצֵק אֲשֶׁר

Matzah that we eat was for what reason? Because the dough of our fathers did not have time to rise before the King of Kings, The Holy One, Blessed is He, revealed Himself to them and redeemed them. Thus it says: *"They baked matzah-cakes from the*

Maggid

הוֹצִיאוּ מִמִּצְרַיִם עֻגֹת מַצּוֹת, כִּי לֹא חָמֵץ, כִּי גֹרְשׁוּ מִמִּצְרַיִם וְלֹא יָכְלוּ לְהִתְמַהְמֵהַּ, וְגַם צֵדָה לֹא עָשׂוּ לָהֶם" (שמות יב:לט).

dough they had brought out of Egypt, because it was not leavened. They were driven out of Egypt and could not delay, and they had also not prepared any provisions."

מָרוֹר זֶה שֶׁאָנוּ אוֹכְלִים, עַל שׁוּם מַה? עַל שׁוּם שֶׁמֵּרְרוּ

This *marror* that we eat, why? Because the Egyptians embit-

As mentioned in the Introduction, the baking of *matzah* was far from incidental. We might have preferred to bake bread but just ran out of time. However, it had been God's plan from the start that the Jewish people specifically bake and eat *matzah*, so that it would be associated with the redemption from Egypt.

This was because *matzah* alludes to the secret of true and lasting freedom. It is simple, like the World to Come, reminding us what life is about from God's perspective.[21] It tells us that though we can enjoy this material world, we should not become overly attached to it. That's when spiritual compromises happen, some of which can trap a person in exile even at the risk of death.

---

[21] *Maharal, Haggadah.*

Maggid

Take the marror into your hand and say:

הַמִּצְרִים אֶת חַיֵּי אֲבוֹתֵינוּ בְּמִצְרַיִם, שֶׁנֶּאֱמַר: "וַיְמָרְרוּ אֶת חַיֵּיהֶם בַּעֲבֹדָה קָשָׁה, בְּחֹמֶר וּבִלְבֵנִים, וּבְכָל עֲבֹדָה בַּשָּׂדֶה, אֵת כָּל עֲבֹדָתָם אֲשֶׁר עָבְדוּ בָהֶם בְּפָרֶךְ" (שמות א:יד).

tered the lives of our ancestors in Egypt, as it is said: *"They made their lives bitter with hard work, with mortar and with bricks, and with all manner of work in the field. They made them do all their work exhaustingly."*

"I'd rather my food be bitter as an olive, but from the hand of God, than as sweet as honey from the hand of men!"[22] That was the message that the dove told Noach by passing over higher and closer trees in search of a sign that the flood was over. It went out of its way to bring back an olive branch for this reason, to say that a relationship with God is worth any bitterness that might occur on occasion.

The message was the same when the Jewish people in the desert arrived at *Marah* in search of much needed water, but found the water bitter.[23] After throwing bitter sticks from an olive tree into the springs, the water became sweet. The

---

[22] *Rashi, Bereishis* 8:11.
[23] *Shemos* 15:23.

message? Remain faithful to God during the "bitter" times, and merit the sweet life it will eventually lead to in this world, and especially in the next one.

The "Four-fifths" that died in the Plague of Darkness didn't get this. Only one fifth of the Jewish population at the time of redemption stayed loyal to God the entire way and merited to leave Egypt. Four-fifths abandoned God and hope of redemption and instead died with the Egyptians. Lest one think this is a message only for past generations, we are told otherwise here:

בְּכָל דּוֹר וָדוֹר חַיָּב אָדָם לִרְאוֹת אֶת עַצְמוֹ כְּאִלּוּ הוּא יָצָא מִמִּצְרַיִם, שֶׁנֶּאֱמַר: "וְהִגַּדְתָּ לְבִנְךָ בַּיּוֹם הַהוּא לֵאמֹר: בַּעֲבוּר זֶה עָשָׂה יְיָ לִי בְּצֵאתִי מִמִּצְרָיִם" (שמות יג:ח).

In every generation a person is obligated to regard himself as if he had come out of Egypt, as it is said: *"You shall tell your child on that day, it is because of this that God did for me when I left Egypt."*

לֹא אֶת אֲבוֹתֵינוּ בִּלְבַד גָּאַל הַקָּדוֹשׁ בָּרוּךְ הוּא, אֶלָּא אַף אוֹתָנוּ גָּאַל עִמָּהֶם, שֶׁנֶּאֱמַר: "וְאוֹתָנוּ הוֹצִיא מִשָּׁם, לְמַעַן הָבִיא אֹתָנוּ, לָתֶת לָנוּ אֶת

The Holy One, Blessed is He, redeemed not only our fathers from Egypt, but He redeemed also us with them, as it is said: *"It was us that He brought out from there, so that He might bring us to give us the land*

Maggid

"הָאָרֶץ אֲשֶׁר נִשְׁבַּע לַאֲבֹתֵנוּ" *that He swore to our fathers.*"
(דברים ו:כג).

If you know the importance of gratitude, then you know the power of praise. The more profound the gratitude is, the more powerful the praise will be. And as a person's sense of gratitude increases, the greater their need will be to release it in praise. It feels very good to sincerely say thank you.

If that is true between people, how much more so is it true between man and God, and even more so the Jewish people and God. We've just finished recounting the many miracles God performed for us just to get us to another *Seder*. By this point, we should be overwhelmed with gratitude, and now we have a chance to direct all that energy where it belongs, towards God. *Hallel* was created for this very reason.

Even though *Hallel* means praise, it also means light.[24] When we say *Hallel* with the proper intention and enthusiasm, we attract additional Divine light towards us, and that means additional blessing. We also radiate with it, which greatly benefits the world around us.

---

[24] *Pesachim* 2a.

Maggid

Cover the matzah and raise the cup. The cup is to be held in the hand until the completion of the blessing, "Who Redeemed Israel."

לְפִיכָךְ אֲנַחְנוּ חַיָּבִים לְהוֹדוֹת, לְהַלֵּל, לְשַׁבֵּחַ, לְפָאֵר, לְרוֹמֵם, לְהַדֵּר, לְבָרֵךְ, לְעַלֵּה וּלְקַלֵּס לְמִי שֶׁעָשָׂה לַאֲבוֹתֵינוּ וְלָנוּ אֶת כָּל הַנִּסִּים הָאֵלּוּ: הוֹצִיאָנוּ מֵעַבְדוּת לְחֵרוּת, מִיָּגוֹן לְשִׂמְחָה, וּמֵאֵבֶל לְיוֹם טוֹב, וּמֵאֲפֵלָה לְאוֹר גָּדוֹל, וּמִשִּׁעְבּוּד לִגְאֻלָּה. וְנֹאמַר לְפָנָיו שִׁירָה חֲדָשָׁה, הַלְלוּיָהּ.

Therefore we are obligated to thank, to laud, to praise, to glorify, to exalt, to adore, to bless, to elevate and to honor the One who did all these miracles for our fathers and for us. He took us from slavery to freedom, from sorrow to joy, and from mourning to festivity, and from deep darkness to great light and from slavery to redemption. Let us say a new song before Him, *Halleluyah!*

הַלְלוּיָהּ! הַלְלוּ עַבְדֵי יְהוָה, הַלְלוּ אֶת שֵׁם יְהוָה. יְהִי שֵׁם יְהוָה מְבֹרָךְ, מֵעַתָּה וְעַד עוֹלָם. מִמִּזְרַח שֶׁמֶשׁ עַד מְבוֹאוֹ, מְהֻלָּל שֵׁם יְהוָה. רָם עַל כָּל גּוֹיִם יְהוָה, עַל הַשָּׁמַיִם כְּבוֹדוֹ. מִי כַּיהוָה אֱלֹהֵינוּ, הַמַּגְבִּיהִי לָשָׁבֶת? הַמַּשְׁפִּילִי לִרְאוֹת,

Halleluyah! Offer praise, servants of God; praise the Name of God. May God's Name be blessed from now and forever. From the rising of the sun to its setting, God's Name is praised. God is high above all nations, His glory is over the heavens. Who is like God, our God, Who

Maggid

בַּשָּׁמַיִם וּבָאָרֶץ? מְקִימִי מֵעָפָר דָּל, מֵאַשְׁפֹּת יָרִים אֶבְיוֹן. לְהוֹשִׁיבִי עִם נְדִיבִים, עִם נְדִיבֵי עַמּוֹ. מוֹשִׁיבִי עֲקֶרֶת הַבַּיִת אֵם הַבָּנִים שְׂמֵחָה. הַלְלוּיָהּ!

בְּצֵאת יִשְׂרָאֵל מִמִּצְרָיִם, בֵּית יַעֲקֹב מֵעַם לֹעֵז. הָיְתָה יְהוּדָה לְקָדְשׁוֹ, יִשְׂרָאֵל מַמְשְׁלוֹתָיו. הַיָּם רָאָה וַיָּנֹס, הַיַּרְדֵּן יִסֹּב לְאָחוֹר. הֶהָרִים רָקְדוּ כְאֵילִים, גְּבָעוֹת כִּבְנֵי צֹאן. מַה לְּךָ הַיָּם כִּי תָנוּס, הַיַּרְדֵּן תִּסֹּב לְאָחוֹר? הֶהָרִים תִּרְקְדוּ כְאֵילִים, גְּבָעוֹת כִּבְנֵי צֹאן? מִלִּפְנֵי אָדוֹן חוּלִי אָרֶץ, מִלִּפְנֵי אֱלוֹהַּ יַעֲקֹב. הַהֹפְכִי הַצּוּר אֲגַם מָיִם, חַלָּמִישׁ לְמַעְיְנוֹ מָיִם.

בָּרוּךְ אַתָּה יְיָ אֱלֹהֵינוּ מֶלֶךְ הָעוֹלָם, אֲשֶׁר גְּאָלָנוּ וְגָאַל אֶת אֲבוֹתֵינוּ מִמִּצְרַיִם, וְהִגִּיעָנוּ

dwells on high yet looks down so low upon Heaven and Earth! He raises the poor from the dust, He lifts the needy from the dunghill, to seat them with nobles, with the nobles of His people. He restores the barren woman to the house, into a joyful mother of children. Halleluyah!

When Israel went out of Egypt, the House of Ya'akov from a people of a foreign language, Yehudah became His holy one, Israel His dominion. The sea saw and fled, the Jordan turned backward. The mountains skipped like rams, the hills like young sheep. What is with you, O sea, that you flee; Jordan, that you turn backward? Mountains, why do you skip like rams; you hills, like young sheep? From before the Master, Who created the earth, from before the God of Ya'akov,

Maggid

לַלַּיְלָה הַזֶּה לֶאֱכָל בּוֹ מַצָּה וּמָרוֹר. כֵּן יְיָ אֱלֹהֵינוּ וֵאלֹהֵי אֲבוֹתֵינוּ יַגִּיעֵנוּ לְמוֹעֲדִים וְלִרְגָלִים אֲחֵרִים הַבָּאִים לִקְרָאתֵנוּ לְשָׁלוֹם, שְׂמֵחִים בְּבִנְיַן עִירֶךָ וְשָׂשִׂים בַּעֲבוֹדָתֶךָ. וְנֹאכַל שָׁם...

רגיל מִן הַזְּבָחִים וּמִן הַפְּסָחִים
במו״ש מִן הַפְּסָחִים וּמִן הַזְּבָחִים

...אֲשֶׁר יַגִּיעַ דָּמָם עַל קִיר מִזְבַּחֲךָ לְרָצוֹן, וְנוֹדֶה לְךָ שִׁיר חָדָשׁ עַל גְּאֻלָּתֵנוּ וְעַל פְּדוּת נַפְשֵׁנוּ. **בָּרוּךְ אַתָּה יְיָ, גָּאַל יִשְׂרָאֵל.**

Who transforms the rock into a pond of water, the flint into a fountain of water.

Blessed are You, God, our God, King of the universe, who has redeemed us and redeemed our fathers from Egypt, and enabled us to attain this night to eat *matzah* and *marror*. So too, God, our God and God of our fathers, enable us to reach other holidays and festivals that will come to us in peace with happiness in the rebuilding of Your city, and with rejoicing in Your service. There we shall eat...

Every night except Saturday Night

of the sacrifices and of the Passover-offerings

On Saturday Night

of the Passover-offerings and of the sacrifices

...whose blood shall be sprinkled on the wall of Your altar for acceptance; and we shall thank You with a new song for our redemption and for the deliverance of our souls. **Blessed are You, God, who redeemed Israel.**

Maggid

Second Cup of Wine

Make the blessing over the second cup (vehitzalti) and drink it while reclining on the left side.

בָּרוּךְ אַתָּה יְיָ אֱלֹהֵינוּ מֶלֶךְ הָעוֹלָם בּוֹרֵא פְּרִי הַגָּפֶן. Blessed are You, God, our God, King of the universe, who creates the fruit of the vine.

This completes the section of *Maggid*, the telling of the story of *Yetzias Mitzrayim*, but it is by no means over. Even the *Hallel* that we started and usually never interrupt for anything, will only be completed after the meal, as if to say that the seudah is not after the telling of the story, but part of it.

For some, the Exodus is just something that happened in the distant past to distant ancestors. *We* tell it, but it is really *their* story. The only relevance it is has to our lives, seemingly to many, is that you can't know where you are going unless you know where you came from.

That might have been true had the story ended with the generation of Jews that left Egypt with Moshe *Rabbeinu*. But it didn't. We left Egypt in Moshe's time, but we have been leaving *Mitzrayim* ever since, and won't have completely left it until *Moshiach* comes and God fills the world with *Da'as Elokim*—Godly Knowledge.

Only then will the *yetzer hara* finally will be gone from mankind, evil from the world, and the blinding veil from Divine Providence. Good and evil, which can be subjective, will once again be replaced with truth and false, which are absolute. The constriction (*meitzer*) of the *Yum*, the *Nun Sha'arei Binah*—the Fifty Gates of Understanding—will be no more.

The Talmud alludes to this by saying that the final redemption will be so great, so awesome that it will make the redemption from Egypt seem very secondary.[25] Like a person who has suffered for years from some illness only to be healed, we will recall *Yetzias Mitzrayim* happening in the past, but only be real with the one that happened in the present.

We should live to celebrate it in our time.

---

[25] *Brochos* 12b.

Rachtzah

רחצה

The hands are washed (twice on the right hand and then twice on the left hand) for matzah and this blessing is said. All wash, but water, basin, and towel are brought for the leader of the Seder to wash at the table. No one should speak until after making the two blessings over the matzah and eating the required amount.

בָּרוּךְ אַתָּה יְיָ אֱלֹהֵינוּ מֶלֶךְ הָעוֹלָם, אֲשֶׁר קִדְּשָׁנוּ בְּמִצְוֹתָיו וְצִוָּנוּ עַל נְטִילַת יָדָיִם.

Blessed are You, God, our God, King of the universe, who has sanctified us with His commandments and commanded us concerning the washing of the hands.

Motzi

מוֹצִיא

Two blessing are said over the matzah, this first one as food about to be enjoyed, and the second for the Torah mitzvah of eating matzah on the first night of Pesach. All the matzos (top whole, the broken middle, and the bottom whole) are taken in hand and raised for this first blessing. The intention should be for the top piece.

בָּרוּךְ אַתָּה יְיָ אֱלֹהֵינוּ מֶלֶךְ הָעוֹלָם, הַמּוֹצִיא לֶחֶם מִן הָאָרֶץ.

Blessed are You, God, our God, King of the universe, Who brings forth bread from the ground.

מַצָּה

Put down the bottom piece of matzah only. For this blessing, the intention should be for the broken piece. Ideally, a kezayis should be broken off from the top piece, and a second kezayis from the middle piece. They should be dipped in salt, and then eaten while reclining on the left side. A person should also have in mind during this blessing the matzah of Korech and the Afikomen.

Everyone at the table should receive a piece from both pieces of matzah. Therefore, additional matzah should be on hand so that everyone obligated in the mitzvah receive at least two kazaysim in total.

The full amount of matzah should be eaten as quickly as possible and without any interruptions, the first kezayis ideally within two to four minute. Unless absolutely necessary, it should also be without drinking anything since it will diminish the taste of the matzah.

Since the prohibition against chometz is so severe, Shemurah Matzah is preferred for all of Pesach, especially for the mitzvah of matzah itself. In addition, barring any halachic health considerations, and at least for this mitzvah, round hand matzos are used as opposed to square machine matzos.

WHY SO STRICT about the amount of *matzah* and time for eating it? Because there is a *mitzvah* to eat *matzah* on the first day of *Pesach* (and the second in the Diaspora), and a *halachic* definition of what is considered an actual eating for the sake of fulfilling the *mitzvah*.[1] Many struggle to comply with the *halachah* because *matzah*, unlike *challah*, is hard and dry, and therefore difficult to chew after a while.

It's quite the quizzical experience for someone complying with the *halachah* for the first time. However, it also tends to add to the authenticity of the *Seder* experience (while

---

[1] *Halachically*, the point of eating is satiation, as the verse says, *"You will eat, be satisfied, and bless God…"* (*Devarim* 8:10). Tradition teaches the amount necessary for this for the average person, which is equal to about 24 grams eaten within two to four minutes, uninterrupted even by speech. Less than this can mean that a person is no longer obligated in a blessing after eating, and *"bentching"* may result in unnecessary blessings (*brochah l'vatalah*).

strengthening jaw muscles), and an opportunity to show a love for *mitzvos*.

Not only this, but *matzah*, according to *Kabbalah*, represents the means of redemption from Egypt. *Matzah* and *chometz* both contain the letters *Mem* and *Tzaddi*, but *matzah* also has a *Heh*, and *chometz*, a *Ches*.

מצה - חמץ

According to *Kabbalah*,[2] while the Jewish people remained in exile the *Heh* of *matzah* was the *Ches* of *chometz*. Redemption occurred when the left leg of the *Ches* was broken into the *Heh* of *matzah*.

Contrary to what many may think, *matzah* is not just unleavened bread, a reminder of our quick departure from Egypt. It is very *kabbalistic* and conceptually special. It's not just *halachah* we fulfill by eating it this way, but we ingest its holy light and radiate it to the world.

The exact amount of matzah that equals the volume of a kezayis (olive) is a point of disagreement,[3] but these are

---

[2] *Biur HaGR"A, Sifra D'Tzniusa,* 26a.

[3] Over time and as a result of changes in nature, we have become unclear about Biblical measurements. We are stringent to cover all bases.

Matzah

accepted amounts for both round hand matzos, considered to be 10.25 inches (26 cm) in diameter, and machine matzos, 6.125 x 7 inches (15.56 x 17.8 cm). The non-bolded numbers are the amounts in case of illness.

	Hand	**Machine**	Hand	Machine
Motzi Matzah	**1/2**	**2/3**	1/4	1/3
Korech	**1/4**	**1/3**	1/4	1/3
Afikomen	**1/2**	**2/3**	1/4	1/3

בָּרוּךְ אַתָּה יְיָ אֱלֹהֵינוּ מֶלֶךְ הָעוֹלָם, אֲשֶׁר קִדְּשָׁנוּ בְּמִצְוֹתָיו, וְצִוָּנוּ עַל אֲכִילַת מַצָּה.

Blessed are You, God, our God, King of the universe, who has sanctified us with His commandments and commanded us concerning the eating of *matzah*.

Marror

מָרוֹר

Take a kezayis (the volume of one olive) of the marror, dip it into the charoses, and then shake off the charoses that stuck to it so that the bitter taste will not be neutralized. Recite the following blessing, but do not lean while eating.

בָּרוּךְ אַתָּה יְיָ אֱלֹהֵינוּ מֶלֶךְ הָעוֹלָם, אֲשֶׁר קִדְּשָׁנוּ בְּמִצְוֹתָיו, וְצִוָּנוּ עַל אֲכִילַת מָרוֹר.

Blessed are You, God, our God, King of the universe, who has sanctified us with His commandments and commanded us concerning the eating of *marror*.

JEWISH HISTORY HAS not all been sweet. In fact, since the beginning when God first made the "Pact of Halves" with Avraham (*Bereishis* 15:9), it was clear that there would be a significant amount of bitterness, starting with personal hardships and continuing into full blown exile and servitude of his descendants.

Not only this, but even after tasting the sweetness of freedom from Egyptian servitude, we were whisked to Mt. Sinai to receive 613 *mitzvos*. We went from human servitude to Divine servitude in 50 short days, and have worked hard to fulfill those *mitzvos* ever since, often in very difficult situations. This has led to statements such as, "It is difficult to be a Jew!"

Anti-Semitism makes it even more difficult to be a Jew. How many times have we been rejected by the gentile world, and often treated worse than animals? Power after power for millennia now has laid waste to *Eretz Yisroel,* and subjugated the Jewish people to exile on and off the land. The Arabs today are just the latest to try.

This has made many Jews over the ages bitter, and has often been cause for some of them to give up on God and being Jewish altogether. They didn't necessarily expect Jewish life to be easy. They just didn't expect it to be so difficult, or so often, and like after eating *marror*, they ended up with a bitter taste in their mouth.

Yet others have persevered, despite the worst *Hashgochah Pratis* and history could throw at them. Despite all the hardship and tests of faith, they remained steadfast in their com-

Marror

mitment to God and traditional Torah values, sometimes losing what mattered most to them in this world. Why? How?

Because they believe this from the Talmud:

Happy are the righteous who receive in this world what is destined for the evil in the World-to-Come. Woe to the evil who receive in this world what is destined for the righteous in the World-to-Come. (*Horayos* 10b)

Righteous people are prepared to sacrifice temporal pleasure in this world for eternal pleasure of the next one. And:

One hour of spiritual bliss in the World-to-Come is better than an entire life in this world. (*Pirkei Avos* 4:17)

But there is more. First, clearly not every Jew has to wait until the World to Come to have pleasure from Torah and *mitzvos*. Many generations, especially ours, have benefited greatly from both even in this world. Second, it is possible to have great spiritual pleasure even without physical pleasure, and sometimes that is the only way. This is why so many people have been willing to sacrifice themselves for what they consider to be noble causes.

Third, we eat Romaine Lettuce at the *Seder* as *marror* because of its bitterness. But we eat it the rest of the year because it is good for us. There are many bitter "pills" that we take because we believe doing so is for our ultimate good.

Marror

The *marror* reminds us that those times that being a Jew becomes like chewing a bitter "pill," we have to recall that ultimately it is for our greater good.

―――――――― Something To Think About ――――――――

The Great Pyramid of Giza is the largest Egyptian pyramid, and like the others, was built primarily by Jewish slaves. Initially standing at 481 feet, the Great Pyramid was the world's tallest human-made structure for more than 3,800 years. The base was measured to be about 755.6 ft square, giving a volume of roughly 92 million cubic feet. The Great Pyramid was built by quarrying an estimated 2.3 million large blocks, weighing six million tons in total.

Korech

כּוֹרֵךְ

Take the third matzah, and also a kezayis of the chazeres dipped into charoses. Combine the two [like a sandwich], and after saying the following, eat them together in the reclining position.

זֵכֶר לְמִקְדָּשׁ כְּהִלֵּל. כֵּן עָשָׂה הִלֵּל בִּזְמַן שֶׁבֵּית הַמִּקְדָּשׁ הָיָה קַיָּם: הָיָה כּוֹרֵךְ (פֶּסַח) מַצָּה וּמָרוֹר וְאוֹכֵל בְּיַחַד, לְקַיֵּם מַה שֶּׁנֶּאֱמַר: "עַל מַצּוֹת וּמְרֹרִים יֹאכְלֻהוּ" (במדבר ט:יא)

A remembrance of the Temple like Hillel did when the Temple stood. He would combine (the *Pesach*,) *matzah* and *marror* and eat them together, as it said: *"They shall eat it with Matzah and bitter herbs."*

IT IS AMAZING how two people can suffer the same difficulty in life, and while one perseveres and survives the other becomes overwhelmed and hopeless. The difference between the two people? Positivity. Though the first person suffers, they hang on because they believe better times will eventually arrive. They might even believe that the today's exile leads to tomorrow's redemption, the message of the *matzah*.

The second person is negative. They might have a good reason for their attitude, but it won't help them solve their current crisis or make their life better. They will tire easily fighting their battle on two fronts, trying to solve the problem while dealing with their anxiety of impending doom. How can they not surrender to their situation? That's the reality of the *marror*.

In truth, everyone goes back-and-forth in life from *matzah* to *marror*, and then back to *matzah* again, etc. But even though life seems like only *matzah* at times, that is, everything goes just right, or *marror*, everything seems to go wrong, life overall is really a "sandwich" of both of them.

The trick is to recall the hope of the *matzah* during the difficult times, and not forget the bitterness of the *marror* during the goods times. Each one tempers the other, providing a person with the kind of balance necessary to remain on spiritual track at all times.

Shulchan Aruch

שֻׁלְחָן עוֹרֵךְ

Now eat and drink to your heart's delight. It is permitted to drink wine between the second and third cups.

What is Yom Tov without a Yom Tov seudah? Eating and drinking always adds to the level of joy, but is always supposed to be a holy and dignified experience. This is especially so for this seudah, since it is also a part of the Seder which is not yet complete. It actually occurs in the middle of Hallel.

For this reason, it is preferable that extraneous conversation be avoided, and that the focus remain on matters of the Haggadah and the story of the exodus. Too often the meal lowers the spiritual level of people eating, when it should actually elevate all those at the table. The goal is freedom from the yetzer hara, not capitulation to it.

It is also important to keep in mind that one should still have an appetite for the Afikomen that follows. Eating on a full stomach does not constitute a halachic eating which can prevent the completion of the mitzvah.

It should be remembered that the main goal of life is to be a means to elevate holy sparks of Divine light from this lowly world to the upper one. Everything in Creation contains such sparks, including food. By eating the proper food in the proper manner, we not only nourish our bodies but nourish our souls with holy sparks, after which they ascend. This leads to Tikun Olam—World Rectification, and a person's portion in the World to Come is built from all the holy sparks—nitzotzei kedushah—they elevated in their lifetime.

As the Talmud says, a person's table is like the mizbayach—altar in the Temple, through which a person atoned for their sins.[1] This only works when a person acts accordingly around it, and behaves like someone made in the image of God.

---

[1] *Chagigah* 27a.

Tzafun

צפון

The Afikoman is the half of the middle matzah that was hidden away to be eaten at the conclusion of the meal. It is not clear if the Afikoman is intended to commemorate the Pesach offering, or the matzah that was eaten together with it. Therefore, ideally one should eat two kezeisim.

Some however find it difficult to eat two kezeisim and therefore eat only one kezayis. If this is the case, the person should have the intention that the kezayis of matzah is for the sake of whichever is the real reason for the Afikoman.

Two kezeisim of matzah should be given to all the participants, which usually means adding additional matzah. The Afikoman should be eaten before Chatzos (halachic midnight), while reclining on the left side, and without pause or interruption (ideally within two to four minutes).

Tzafun

After the Afikoman has been eaten, a person should not eat or drink anything else other the remaining two cups of wine. This is so that the taste of the matzah will remain in the mouth. Water is permissible if necessary.

TZAFUN MEANS HIDDEN, like in the verse:

How great is Your goodness that You have hidden away—tzafanta—for those who fear You, that You have worked for those who take refuge in You, in the presence of the sons of men! (*Tehillim* 31:20)

And after Yosef successfully interpreted Pharaoh's dreams and promoted him to viceroy, it says:

Pharaoh named Yosef, "Tzafnas Panayach"... (*Bereishis* 41:45)

which *Rashi* says means, "He who explains hidden things" which, in this case, referred to God's plans for Egypt.

The *Talmud Bavli* explains that the word *Afikoman* derives from the Greek word for "dessert," which the last thing eaten at a meal. The *Talmud Yerushalmi* however says that the word is derived from *epikomion*, meaning "after-dinner entertainment." Either way, why use a Greek word at such a seminal Jewish event that carries with it one of the most seminal Jewish messages?

Tzafun

Remember the *Rasha,* the Evil Son? What was really bothering him that he asked his question? He had a difficult time fitting his Jewish heritage into his modern life. Like so many Jews before and after him, he was attracted to the world around him, and as that attraction grew, so did his desire to turn his back on Torah Judaism.

"There is nothing new under the sun." Chava, in the Garden of Eden, was attracted by the fruit of the *Aitz HaDa'as Tov v'Ra*, the Tree of Knowledge of Good and Evil, over the *hidden* fruit of the *Aitz HaChaim*, the Tree of Life. And mankind has been making the same mistake ever since, investing so much in knowledge they can see and immediately use, over knowledge they have to pursue and discover.

This approach to life infiltrated the Jewish people during the time of the Greeks. Over time, many Jews were drawn to the Greek way of life and became *Misyavnim*—Hellenists. The trend has continued ever since and only worsened with time, causing many to either leave Judaism altogether, or make it only ceremonial.

Tzafun is the parting message of the *Haggadah*. It tells us that God's truth is something you have to go in search of, and not to settle for half-baked truths that promise instant gratification. Be patient, do your due diligence, and be amazed at what you uncover, in *this* world and especially in

Tzafun

the next world.

The true "*Afikomen*" in life is not what the "Greeks" serve up. It is what the Torah has prepared for the person who seeks it out like "buried treasures," and makes the incredible journey through *Pardes,* the Paradise man has been trying to return to ever since Adam and Chava first made their mistake.

———————— Something To Think About ————————

The Korban Pesach is *kodshim kalim*, and had to be eaten within the walls of Jerusalem. People from all over *Eretz Yisroel* came, as well large groups came from Bavel. King Agrippas took a census, and the total was 12,000,000 people in *Yerushalayim* eating the korban (*Pesachim* 64b)! Everyone had to immerse in a *mikvah* before entering the Temple, and to facilitate the flow of people *mikvaos* were built with two sets of stairs, one for entering and one for exiting. Assuming it took a minimum of ten seconds to go down, immerse and come up, it would require over 3,000 hours for millions to immerse! The *Sanhedrin* required all cattle dealers in the area to bring their animals so they should be available for purchase. According to a Roman living during the time of the second Temple, a person could not see the grass on the hills surrounding *Yerushalayim* because of the multitude of animals.

Barech

בָּרֵךְ

The third cup is poured and Birchas HaMazon (Grace After Meals) is said. Some have the custom to pour the Kos Shel Eliyahu—Cup of Eliyahu—at this time.

WE ARE TOLD in the Torah to *"eat, be satiated, and bless God your God."*[1] We are told by the Talmud that this halachah began as a tradition going back to Avraham *Avinu*:

This teaches that Avraham *Avinu* caused the name of The Holy One, Blessed is He, to be called out in the mouth of all passersby. How? After the guests of Avraham ate and drank, they got up to bless him. He said to them: "Did you eat from what is mine? You ate from the food of the God of the world,

---

[1] *Devarim* 8:10.

Barech

and therefore, you should thank and praise and bless the One Who spoke and the world was created." (*Sotah* 10b)

It was more than just a nice thing that Avraham did. It was how he reconnected mankind with God...and happened to save the world from another destruction. By showing how sustenance was a miracle and not to be take for granted, Avraham made God reality for others who treated it like myth.

Nothing has changed over the millennia. If anything, the situation worsened once technology gave man more control over the production of his food. This has increased the disconnect between man and God, which can't be good. God is extremely patient, but only for so long...and it already has been so long.

This is why it is important not only to "*bentch*," but to do so with intent and great sincerity. We're not just saying thank you for our food, which is reason enough to *bentch*. We're connecting to God through *bentching*, and saving the world at the same time.

The third cup of wine is poured at this time, and Birchas HaMazon *is recited over it. Hold the cup like you would for* Kiddush *until after the words, "and may He never cause us to lack any good."*

Barech

Birchas HaMazon

שִׁיר הַמַּעֲלוֹת: בְּשׁוּב יְהוָה אֶת שִׁיבַת צִיּוֹן, הָיִינוּ כְּחֹלְמִים. אָז יִמָּלֵא שְׂחוֹק פִּינוּ וּלְשׁוֹנֵנוּ רִנָּה. אָז יֹאמְרוּ בַגּוֹיִם: הִגְדִּיל יְהוָה לַעֲשׂוֹת עִם אֵלֶּה. הִגְדִּיל יְהוָה לַעֲשׂוֹת עִמָּנוּ, הָיִינוּ שְׂמֵחִים. שׁוּבָה יְהוָה אֶת שְׁבִיתֵנוּ, כַּאֲפִיקִים בַּנֶּגֶב. הַזֹּרְעִים בְּדִמְעָה, בְּרִנָּה יִקְצֹרוּ. הָלוֹךְ יֵלֵךְ וּבָכֹה נֹשֵׂא מֶשֶׁךְ הַזָּרַע, בֹּא יָבוֹא בְרִנָּה נֹשֵׂא אֲלֻמֹּתָיו. (תהלים קכו)

A Song of Ascents. When God will return the exiles of Tzion, we will have been like dreamers. Then our mouth will be filled with laughter, and our tongue with joyous song. Then will they say among the nations, "God has done great things for these." God has done great things for us, we were joyful. God, return our exiles as streams in the Negev. Those who sow in tears will reap with joyous song. He goes along weeping, carrying the bag of seed; he will surely come [back] with joyous song, carrying his sheaves.

Mayim Acharonim (After Waters) is washed at this time, after which no one should speak until after *Birchas HaMazon* has been completed. If three to nine males over the age of 13 are *bentching* together, the one leading should begin with the following.

115

Barech

If there are ten or more males over 13 *bentching* together, the bracketed "*Elokim*" is also included.

הַמְזַמֵן: רַבּוֹתַי, נְבָרֵךְ.

הַמְסֻבִּים: יְהִי שֵׁם יְיָ מְבֹרָךְ מֵעַתָּה וְעַד עוֹלָם.

הַמְזַמֵן: יְהִי שֵׁם יְיָ מְבֹרָךְ מֵעַתָּה וְעַד עוֹלָם. בִּרְשׁוּת מָרָנָן וְרַבָּנָן וְרַבּוֹתַי, נְבָרֵךְ (בעשרה: אֱלֹהֵינוּ) שֶׁאָכַלְנוּ מִשֶּׁלּוֹ.

הַמְסֻבִּים: בָּרוּךְ (אֱלֹהֵינוּ) שֶׁאָכַלְנוּ מִשֶּׁלּוֹ וּבְטוּבוֹ חָיִינוּ.

הַמְזַמֵן: בָּרוּךְ (אֱלֹהֵינוּ) שֶׁאָכַלְנוּ מִשֶּׁלּוֹ וּבְטוּבוֹ חָיִינוּ.

Leader: Gentlemen, let us say Grace!

Others: May the Name of God be blessed from now and forever.

Leader: May the Name of God be blessed from now and forever...With the permission of the masters, teachers and gentlemen, let us bless He (if 10 or more: *our God* instead of "He") of whose bounty we have eaten.

Others: Blessed be He (if 10 or more: *our God* instead of "He") of whose bounty we have eaten, and through whose goodness we live.

Leader: Blessed be He (if 10 or more: *our God* instead of "He") of whose bounty we have eaten, and through whose goodness we live.

Barech

בָּרוּךְ אַתָּה יְיָ אֱלֹהֵינוּ מֶלֶךְ הָעוֹלָם, הַזָּן אֶת הָעוֹלָם כֻּלּוֹ בְּטוּבוֹ בְּחֵן בְּחֶסֶד וּבְרַחֲמִים. הוּא נוֹתֵן לֶחֶם לְכָל בָּשָׂר כִּי לְעוֹלָם חַסְדּוֹ. וּבְטוּבוֹ הַגָּדוֹל, תָּמִיד לֹא חָסַר לָנוּ, וְאַל יֶחְסַר לָנוּ מָזוֹן לְעוֹלָם וָעֶד. בַּעֲבוּר שְׁמוֹ הַגָּדוֹל, כִּי הוּא אֵל זָן וּמְפַרְנֵס לַכֹּל, וּמֵטִיב לַכֹּל, וּמֵכִין מָזוֹן לְכָל בְּרִיּוֹתָיו אֲשֶׁר בָּרָא. (כָּאָמוּר: פּוֹתֵחַ אֶת יָדֶךָ, וּמַשְׂבִּיעַ לְכָל חַי רָצוֹן). בָּרוּךְ אַתָּה יְיָ הַזָּן אֶת הַכֹּל.

נוֹדֶה לְךָ יְיָ אֱלֹהֵינוּ עַל שֶׁהִנְחַלְתָּ לַאֲבוֹתֵינוּ אֶרֶץ חֶמְדָּה טוֹבָה וּרְחָבָה, וְעַל שֶׁהוֹצֵאתָנוּ יְיָ אֱלֹהֵינוּ מֵאֶרֶץ מִצְרַיִם, וּפְדִיתָנוּ מִבֵּית עֲבָדִים, וְעַל בְּרִיתְךָ שֶׁחָתַמְתָּ בִּבְשָׂרֵנוּ, וְעַל תּוֹרָתְךָ שֶׁלִּמַּדְתָּנוּ, וְעַל חֻקֶּיךָ שֶׁהוֹדַעְתָּנוּ, וְעַל חַיִּים, חֵן וָחֶסֶד שֶׁחוֹנַנְתָּנוּ,

Blessed are You, God, our God, King of the universe, who, in His goodness, feeds the whole world with grace, with kindness and with mercy. He gives food to all flesh, for His kindness is everlasting. Through His great goodness to us continuously we do not lack food, and may we never lack it, for the sake of His great Name. For He is a [benevolent] God who feeds and sustains all, does good to all, and prepares food for all His creatures whom He has created, (as it is said: You open Your hand and satisfy the desire of every living thing). Blessed are You God, who provides food for all.

We thank You, God, our God, for having given as a heritage to our fathers a precious, good and spacious land; for having brought us out, God our God,

Barech

from the land of Egypt and redeemed us from the house of slaves; for Your covenant which You have sealed in our flesh; for Your Torah which You have taught us; for Your statutes which You have made known to us; for the life, favor and kindness which You have graciously bestowed upon us; and for the food we eat with which You constantly feed and sustain us every day, at all times, and at every hour.

For all this, God our God, we thank You and bless You. May Your Name be blessed by the mouth of every living being, constantly and forever. As it is written: When you have eaten and are satiated, you shall bless God your God, for the good land which He has given you. Blessed are You, God, for the land and for the food.

Have mercy, God our God,

וְעַל אֲכִילַת מָזוֹן שָׁאַתָּה זָן וּמְפַרְנֵס אוֹתָנוּ תָּמִיד, בְּכָל יוֹם וּבְכָל עֵת וּבְכָל שָׁעָה.

וְעַל הַכֹּל יְיָ אֱלֹהֵינוּ אֲנַחְנוּ מוֹדִים לָךְ וּמְבָרְכִים אוֹתָךְ, יִתְבָּרַךְ שִׁמְךָ בְּפִי כָּל חַי תָּמִיד לְעוֹלָם וָעֶד. כַּכָּתוּב: וְאָכַלְתָּ וְשָׂבָעְתָּ, וּבֵרַכְתָּ אֶת יְיָ אֱלֹהֶיךָ עַל הָאָרֶץ הַטֹּבָה אֲשֶׁר נָתַן לָךְ. בָּרוּךְ אַתָּה יְיָ עַל הָאָרֶץ וְעַל הַמָּזוֹן.

רַחֵם נָא יְיָ אֱלֹהֵינוּ עַל יִשְׂרָאֵל עַמֶּךָ וְעַל יְרוּשָׁלַיִם עִירֶךָ וְעַל צִיּוֹן מִשְׁכַּן כְּבוֹדֶךָ וְעַל מַלְכוּת בֵּית דָּוִד מְשִׁיחֶךָ וְעַל הַבַּיִת הַגָּדוֹל וְהַקָּדוֹשׁ שֶׁנִּקְרָא שִׁמְךָ עָלָיו. אֱלֹהֵינוּ, אָבִינוּ, רְעֵנוּ זוּנֵנוּ פַּרְנְסֵנוּ וְכַלְכְּלֵנוּ וְהַרְוִיחֵנוּ, וְהַרְוַח לָנוּ יְיָ אֱלֹהֵינוּ מְהֵרָה מִכָּל צָרוֹתֵינוּ. וְנָא אַל תַּצְרִיכֵנוּ יְיָ

Barech

אֱלֹהֵינוּ, לֹא לִידֵי מַתְּנַת בָּשָׂר וָדָם וְלֹא לִידֵי הַלְוָאָתָם, כִּי אִם לְיָדְךָ הַמְּלֵאָה הַפְּתוּחָה הַקְּדוֹשָׁה וְהָרְחָבָה, שֶׁלֹּא נֵבוֹשׁ וְלֹא נִכָּלֵם לְעוֹלָם וָעֶד.

בְּשַׁבָּת

רְצֵה וְהַחֲלִיצֵנוּ יְיָ אֱלֹהֵינוּ בְּמִצְוֹתֶיךָ וּבְמִצְוַת יוֹם הַשְּׁבִיעִי הַשַּׁבָּת הַגָּדוֹל וְהַקָּדוֹשׁ הַזֶּה. כִּי יוֹם זֶה גָּדוֹל וְקָדוֹשׁ הוּא לְפָנֶיךָ, לִשְׁבָּת בּוֹ וְלָנוּחַ בּוֹ בְּאַהֲבָה כְּמִצְוַת רְצוֹנֶךָ. וּבִרְצוֹנְךָ הָנִיחַ לָנוּ יְיָ אֱלֹהֵינוּ שֶׁלֹּא תְהֵא צָרָה וְיָגוֹן וַאֲנָחָה בְּיוֹם מְנוּחָתֵנוּ. וְהַרְאֵנוּ יְיָ אֱלֹהֵינוּ בְּנֶחָמַת צִיּוֹן עִירֶךָ, וּבְבִנְיַן יְרוּשָׁלַיִם עִיר קָדְשֶׁךָ, כִּי אַתָּה הוּא בַּעַל הַיְשׁוּעוֹת וּבַעַל הַנֶּחָמוֹת.

upon Israel Your people, upon Jerusalem Your city, upon Tzion the abode of Your glory, upon the kingship of the house of David Your anointed, and upon the great and holy House which is called by Your Name. Our God, our Father, Our Shepherd, feed us, sustain us, nourish us and give us comfort; and speedily, God our God, grant us relief from all our afflictions. God, our God, please do not make us dependent upon the gifts of mortal men nor upon their loans, but only upon Your full, open, holy and generous hand, that we may not be shamed or disgraced forever and ever.

On *Shabbos*

May it please You, God, our God, to strengthen us through Your commandments, and through the precept of the

Barech

אֱלֹהֵינוּ וֵאלֹהֵי אֲבוֹתֵינוּ, יַעֲלֶה וְיָבֹא וְיַגִּיעַ וְיֵרָאֶה וְיֵרָצֶה וְיִשָּׁמַע וְיִפָּקֵד וְיִזָּכֵר זִכְרוֹנֵנוּ וּפִקְדּוֹנֵנוּ, וְזִכְרוֹן אֲבוֹתֵינוּ, וְזִכְרוֹן מָשִׁיחַ בֶּן דָּוִד עַבְדֶּךָ, וְזִכְרוֹן יְרוּשָׁלַיִם עִיר קָדְשֶׁךָ, וְזִכְרוֹן כָּל עַמְּךָ בֵּית יִשְׂרָאֵל לְפָנֶיךָ, לִפְלֵיטָה, לְטוֹבָה, לְחֵן וּלְחֶסֶד וּלְרַחֲמִים, לְחַיִּים וּלְשָׁלוֹם, בְּיוֹם חַג הַמַּצּוֹת הַזֶּה. זָכְרֵנוּ יְיָ אֱלֹהֵינוּ בּוֹ לְטוֹבָה, וּפָקְדֵנוּ בוֹ לִבְרָכָה, וְהוֹשִׁיעֵנוּ בוֹ לְחַיִּים (טוֹבִים). וּבִדְבַר יְשׁוּעָה וְרַחֲמִים חוּס וְחָנֵּנוּ וְרַחֵם עָלֵינוּ וְהוֹשִׁיעֵנוּ, כִּי אֵלֶיךָ עֵינֵינוּ, כִּי אֵל מֶלֶךְ חַנּוּן וְרַחוּם אָתָּה.

וּבְנֵה יְרוּשָׁלַיִם עִיר הַקֹּדֶשׁ בִּמְהֵרָה בְיָמֵינוּ. בָּרוּךְ אַתָּה יְיָ בּוֹנֵה בְרַחֲמָיו יְרוּשָׁלָיִם. אָמֵן.

Seventh Day, this great and holy *Shabbos*. For this day is great and holy before You, to refrain from work and to rest thereon with love, in accordance with the commandment of Your will. In Your will, God, our God, bestow upon us tranquility, that there shall be no trouble, sadness or grief on the day of our rest. God, our God, let us see the consolation of *Tzion* Your city, and the rebuilding of Jerusalem Your holy city, for You are the Master of [all] salvations and the Master of [all] consolations.]

Our God and God of our fathers, may there ascend, come and reach, be seen and accepted, heard, recalled and remembered before You, the remembrance and recollection of us, the remembrance of our fathers, the remembrance of *Moshiach Ben David* Your

Barech

בָּרוּךְ אַתָּה יְיָ אֱלֹהֵינוּ מֶלֶךְ הָעוֹלָם, הָאֵל אָבִינוּ מַלְכֵּנוּ אַדִירֵנוּ בּוֹרְאֵנוּ גֹּאֲלֵנוּ יוֹצְרֵנוּ קְדוֹשֵׁנוּ, קְדוֹשׁ יַעֲקֹב, רוֹעֵנוּ, רוֹעֵה יִשְׂרָאֵל, הַמֶּלֶךְ הַטּוֹב וְהַמֵּטִיב לַכֹּל, שֶׁבְּכָל יוֹם וָיוֹם הוּא הֵטִיב, הוּא מֵטִיב, הוּא יֵיטִיב לָנוּ. הוּא גְמָלָנוּ הוּא גוֹמְלֵנוּ הוּא יִגְמְלֵנוּ לָעַד, לְחֵן וּלְחֶסֶד וּלְרַחֲמִים, וּלְרֶוַח הַצָּלָה וְהַצְלָחָה, בְּרָכָה וִישׁוּעָה, נֶחָמָה פַּרְנָסָה וְכַלְכָּלָה, וְרַחֲמִים וְחַיִּים וְשָׁלוֹם וְכָל טוֹב, וּמִכָּל טוּב לְעוֹלָם עַל יְחַסְּרֵנוּ.

הָרַחֲמָן הוּא יִמְלוֹךְ עָלֵינוּ לְעוֹלָם וָעֶד.

הָרַחֲמָן הוּא יִתְבָּרַךְ בַּשָּׁמַיִם וּבָאָרֶץ.

הָרַחֲמָן הוּא יִשְׁתַּבַּח לְדוֹר דּוֹרִים, וְיִתְפָּאַר בָּנוּ לָעַד

servant, the remembrance of Jerusalem Your holy city, and the remembrance of all Your people the House of Israel, for deliverance, well-being, grace, kindness, mercy, good life and peace, on this day of the Festival of *Matzos*, on this Festival of holy convocation. Remember us on this [day], God, our God, for good; recollect us on this [day] for blessing; help us on this [day] for good life. With the promise of deliverance and compassion, spare us and be gracious to us; have mercy upon us and deliver us; for our eyes are directed to You, for You, God, are a gracious and merciful King.

Rebuild Jerusalem the holy city speedily in our days. Blessed are You, God, who in His mercy rebuilds Jerusalem. Amen.

Blessed are You, God, our God, King of the universe,

Barech

benevolent God, our Father, our King, our Might, our Creator, our Redeemer, our Maker, our Holy One, the Holy One of Ya'akov, our Shepherd, the Shepherd of Israel, the King who is good and does good to all, each and every day. He has done good for us, He does good for us, and He will do good for us; He has bestowed, He bestows, and He will forever bestow upon us grace, kindness and mercy, relief, salvation and success, blessing and help, consolation, sustenance and nourishment, compassion, life, peace and all goodness; and may He never cause us to lack any good.

May the Merciful One reign over us forever and ever.

May the Merciful One be blessed in heaven and on earth.

וּלְנֶצַח נְצָחִים, וְיִתְהַדַּר בָּנוּ לָעַד וּלְעוֹלְמֵי עוֹלָמִים.

הָרַחֲמָן הוּא יְפַרְנְסֵנוּ בְּכָבוֹד.

הָרַחֲמָן הוּא יִשְׁבּוֹר עֻלֵּנוּ מֵעַל צַוָּארֵנוּ, וְהוּא יוֹלִיכֵנוּ קוֹמְמִיּוּת לְאַרְצֵנוּ.

הָרַחֲמָן הוּא יִשְׁלַח לָנוּ בְּרָכָה מְרֻבָּה בַּבַּיִת הַזֶּה, וְעַל שֻׁלְחָן זֶה שֶׁאָכַלְנוּ עָלָיו.

הָרַחֲמָן הוּא יִשְׁלַח לָנוּ אֶת אֵלִיָּהוּ הַנָּבִיא זָכוּר לַטּוֹב, וִיבַשֶּׂר לָנוּ בְּשׂוֹרוֹת טוֹבוֹת יְשׁוּעוֹת וְנֶחָמוֹת.

הָרַחֲמָן הוּא יְבָרֵךְ אֶת (אָבִי מוֹרִי) בַּעַל הַבַּיִת הַזֶּה, וְאֶת (אִמִּי מוֹרָתִי) בַּעֲלַת הַבַּיִת הַזֶּה, אוֹתָם וְאֶת בֵּיתָם וְאֶת זַרְעָם וְאֶת כָּל אֲשֶׁר לָהֶם.

Barech

אוֹתָנוּ וְאֶת כָּל אֲשֶׁר לָנוּ, כְּמוֹ שֶׁנִּתְבָּרְכוּ אֲבוֹתֵינוּ אַבְרָהָם יִצְחָק וְיַעֲקֹב: בַּכֹּל מִכֹּל כֹּל. כֵּן יְבָרֵךְ אוֹתָנוּ כֻּלָּנוּ יַחַד בִּבְרָכָה שְׁלֵמָה, וְנֹאמַר: אָמֵן.

בַּמָּרוֹם יְלַמְּדוּ עֲלֵיהֶם וְעָלֵינוּ זְכוּת שֶׁתְּהֵא לְמִשְׁמֶרֶת שָׁלוֹם. וְנִשָּׂא בְרָכָה מֵאֵת יְיָ, וּצְדָקָה מֵאֱלֹהֵי יִשְׁעֵנוּ, וְנִמְצָא חֵן וְשֵׂכֶל טוֹב בְּעֵינֵי אֱלֹהִים וְאָדָם.

בְּשַׁבָּת: **הָרַחֲמָן** הוּא יַנְחִילֵנוּ יוֹם שֶׁכֻּלּוֹ שַׁבָּת וּמְנוּחָה לְחַיֵּי הָעוֹלָמִים.

הָרַחֲמָן הוּא יַנְחִילֵנוּ לְיוֹם שֶׁכֻּלּוֹ טוֹב. (לְיוֹם שֶׁכֻּלּוֹ אָרוֹךְ. יוֹם שֶׁצַּדִּיקִים יוֹשְׁבִים וְעַטְרוֹתֵיהֶם בְּרָאשֵׁיהֶם

May the Merciful One be praised for all generations, and be glorified in us forever and all eternity, and honored in us forever and ever.

May the Merciful One sustain us with honor.

May the Merciful One break the yoke of exile from our neck and may He lead us upright to our land.

May the Merciful One send abundant blessing into this house and upon this table at which we have eaten.

May the Merciful One send us Eliyahu *HaNavi,* may he be remembered for good, and may he bring us good tidings, salvation and consolation.

May the Merciful One bless my father, my teacher, the master of this house, and my mother, my teacher, the mistress of this house; them, their household,

123

Barech

their children, and all that is theirs; us, and all that is ours. Just as He blessed our forefathers, Avraham, Yitzchak and Ya'akov, in everything, from everything, with everything, so may He bless all of us (the children of the Covenant) together with a perfect blessing, and let us say, Amen.

From On High, may there be invoked upon him and upon us such merit which will bring a safeguarding of peace. May we receive blessing from God and just kindness from the God of our salvation, and may we find grace and good understanding in the eyes of God and man.

On *Shabbos*: **May** the Merciful One cause us to inherit that day which will be all *Shabbos* and rest for life everlasting.

May the Merciful One cause us to inherit that day which is

וְנֶהֱנִים מִזִּיו הַשְּׁכִינָה, וִיהִי חֶלְקֵנוּ עִמָּהֶם)

הָרַחֲמָן הוּא יְזַכֵּנוּ לִימוֹת הַמָּשִׁיחַ וּלְחַיֵּי הָעוֹלָם הַבָּא. מִגְדּוֹל יְשׁוּעוֹת מַלְכּוֹ, וְעֹשֶׂה חֶסֶד לִמְשִׁיחוֹ, לְדָוִד וּלְזַרְעוֹ עַד עוֹלָם.

עֹשֶׂה שָׁלוֹם בִּמְרוֹמָיו, הוּא יַעֲשֶׂה שָׁלוֹם עָלֵינוּ וְעַל כָּל יִשְׂרָאֵל, וְאִמְרוּ: אָמֵן.

יְראוּ אֶת יְיָ קְדֹשָׁיו, כִּי אֵין מַחְסוֹר לִירֵאָיו. כְּפִירִים רָשׁוּ וְרָעֵבוּ, וְדֹרְשֵׁי יְיָ לֹא יַחְסְרוּ כָל טוֹב. הוֹדוּ לַייָ כִּי טוֹב, כִּי לְעוֹלָם חַסְדּוֹ. פּוֹתֵחַ אֶת יָדֶךָ, וּמַשְׂבִּיעַ לְכָל חַי רָצוֹן. בָּרוּךְ הַגֶּבֶר אֲשֶׁר יִבְטַח בַּייָ, וְהָיָה יְיָ מִבְטַחוֹ. נַעַר הָיִיתִי גַּם זָקַנְתִּי, וְלֹא רָאִיתִי צַדִּיק נֶעֱזָב וְזַרְעוֹ מְבַקֶּשׁ לָחֶם. יְיָ עֹז לְעַמּוֹ יִתֵּן, יְיָ יְבָרֵךְ אֶת עַמּוֹ בַשָּׁלוֹם.

Barech

all good.

May the Merciful One grant us the privilege of reaching the days of *Moshiach* and the life of the World to Come. He is a tower of salvation to His king, and bestows kindness upon His anointed, to David and his descendants forever. He who makes peace in His heights, may He make peace for us and for all Israel; and say, Amen.

Fear God, you His holy ones, for those who fear Him suffer no want. Young lions are in need and go hungry, but those who seek God shall not lack any good. Give thanks to God for He is good, for His kindness is everlasting. You open Your hand and satisfy the desire of every living thing. Blessed is the man who trusts in God, and God will be his trust. I have been young and now I am old, yet have I not seen the righteous forsaken, nor his seed begging for bread. God will give strength unto his people; God will bless his people with peace.

Recite the blessing for the third cup (vega'alti) and drink it while reclining to the left..

בָּרוּךְ אַתָּה יְיָ אֱלֹהֵינוּ מֶלֶךְ הָעוֹלָם, בּוֹרֵא פְּרִי הַגָפֶן.

Blessed are You, God, our God, King of the universe, who creates the fruit of the vine.

Hallel

The fourth cup is poured and the door is opened, and this is said:

שְׁפֹךְ חֲמָתְךָ אֶל הַגּוֹיִם אֲשֶׁר לֹא יְדָעוּךָ וְעַל מַמְלָכוֹת אֲשֶׁר בְּשִׁמְךָ לֹא קָרָאוּ. כִּי אָכַל אֶת יַעֲקֹב וְאֶת נָוֵהוּ הֵשַׁמּוּ. (תהלים עט ו-ז) שְׁפֹךְ עֲלֵיהֶם זַעְמֶךָ, וַחֲרוֹן אַפְּךָ יַשִּׂיגֵם. (תהלים סט:כה) תִּרְדֹּף בְּאַף וְתַשְׁמִידֵם מִתַּחַת שְׁמֵי יְיָ. (איכה ג:סו)

Pour out Your wrath upon the nations that do not acknowledge You, and upon the kingdoms that do not call upon Your Name. *"For they have devoured Ya'akov and laid waste his habitation." "Pour out Your indignation upon them, and let the wrath of Your anger overtake them." "Pursue them with anger, and destroy them from beneath the heavens of God."*

Hallel

IT'S A VERY strong and dramatic declaration we make at this time, one that seems to belong on the other side of the *seudah*, not here. The first part of the *Seder* built momentum and fervor which, more than likely, has dissipated by the end of the meal and after *bentching*. We have been satiated spiritually and physically, making it harder to feel the import of these words.

If, that is, we are talking about vengeance on behalf of the Jewish people. If we are fortunate enough to be making a *Seder* in the comfort and security of our own homes (and how much so if in *Eretz Yisroel*), and to have all the components necessary to make a complete *Seder*, then vengeance is probably the last thing on our minds.

But we are not talking about vengeance for the thousands of years of cruelty to the Jewish people. We are talking about vengeance for God, for how the nations of the world have ignored Him and abused His world. Like Pinchas in *Shittim*,[1] we are jealous on behalf of *God*, not *ourselves,* and that is something we need to be no matter what our situation is.

Because, as long as the *Shechinah* is in exile, the Temple is in ruins, and Jews are scattered around the world, no *simchah* is complete. Even worse, it is a *Chillul Hashem*, a profana-

---

[1] *Bamidbar* 25:1.

Hallel

tion of God's name, regarding which the prophet has said:

And they entered the nations where they came, and they profaned My Holy Name, because it was said of them, "These are the people of God, and they have come out of His land." But I had pity on My Holy Name, which the House of Israel had profaned among the nations to which they had come. Therefore, tell the House of Israel: "God says: 'Not for your sake do I do this, House of Israel, but for My Holy Name, which you have profaned among the nations to which they have come. And I will sanctify My great Name…because I will take you from among the nations and gather you from all the countries, and I will bring you to your land.'" (Yechezkel 36:21-24)

The *seudah* may be over, the *Seder* may be reaching its yearly end, and we may be satisfied with all that we have been able to accomplish while in exile. But we can never lose sight of how the *Shechinah* suffers all through exile, for God's sake and our own. We have seen too many times how exiles we treat like redemptions can come to an abrupt end, and how all that was accomplished can come down faster than it went up.

With all of that in mind, we are now ready to complete *Hallel* with a full and sincere heart.

Hallel

לֹא לָנוּ יְהוָה לֹא לָנוּ, כִּי לְשִׁמְךָ תֵּן כָּבוֹד, עַל חַסְדְּךָ עַל אֲמִתֶּךָ. לָמָּה יֹאמְרוּ הַגּוֹיִם אַיֵּה נָא אֱלֹהֵיהֶם. וֵאלֹהֵינוּ בַשָּׁמָיִם, כֹּל אֲשֶׁר חָפֵץ עָשָׂה. עֲצַבֵּיהֶם כֶּסֶף וְזָהָב, מַעֲשֵׂה יְדֵי אָדָם. פֶּה לָהֶם וְלֹא יְדַבֵּרוּ, עֵינַיִם לָהֶם וְלֹא יִרְאוּ. אָזְנַיִם לָהֶם וְלֹא יִשְׁמָעוּ, אַף לָהֶם וְלֹא יְרִיחוּן. יְדֵיהֶם וְלֹא יְמִישׁוּן, רַגְלֵיהֶם וְלֹא יְהַלֵּכוּ, לֹא יֶהְגּוּ בִּגְרוֹנָם. כְּמוֹהֶם יִהְיוּ עֹשֵׂיהֶם, כֹּל אֲשֶׁר בֹּטֵחַ בָּהֶם. יִשְׂרָאֵל בְּטַח בַּיהוָה עֶזְרָם וּמָגִנָּם הוּא. בֵּית אַהֲרֹן בִּטְחוּ בַיהוָה עֶזְרָם וּמָגִנָּם הוּא. יִרְאֵי יְהוָה בִּטְחוּ בַיהוָה עֶזְרָם וּמָגִנָּם הוּא.

Not to us, God, not to us, but to Your Name give glory, for the sake of Your kindness and Your truth. Why should the nations say, "Where is their God now?" Our God is in Heaven, and whatever He desires, He does. Their idols are of silver and gold, the product of human hands. They have a mouth, but cannot speak; they have eyes, but cannot see; they have ears, but cannot hear; they have a nose, but cannot smell; their hands cannot feel; their feet cannot walk; they can make no sound with their throat. Their makers should be like them, everyone that trusts in them. Israel, trust in God! He is their help and their shield. House of Aharon, trust in God! He is their help and their shield. You who fear God, trust in God! He is their help and their shield.

יְהוָה זְכָרָנוּ יְבָרֵךְ. יְבָרֵךְ אֶת בֵּית יִשְׂרָאֵל, יְבָרֵךְ אֶת בֵּית

God, mindful of us, will bless. He will bless the House of Is-

Hallel

אַהֲרֹן, יְבָרֵךְ יִרְאֵי יְהֹוָה, הַקְּטַנִּים עִם הַגְּדֹלִים. יֹסֵף יְהֹוָה עֲלֵיכֶם, עֲלֵיכֶם וְעַל בְּנֵיכֶם. טוֹ בְּרוּכִים אַתֶּם לַיהֹוָה, עֹשֵׂה שָׁמַיִם וָאָרֶץ. הַשָּׁמַיִם, שָׁמַיִם לַיהֹוָה, וְהָאָרֶץ נָתַן לִבְנֵי אָדָם. לֹא הַמֵּתִים יְהַלְלוּ יָהּ, וְלֹא כָּל יֹרְדֵי דוּמָה. וַאֲנַחְנוּ נְבָרֵךְ יָהּ, מֵעַתָּה וְעַד עוֹלָם. הַלְלוּיָהּ.

אָהַבְתִּי כִּי יִשְׁמַע יְהֹוָה אֶת קוֹלִי תַּחֲנוּנָי. כִּי הִטָּה אָזְנוֹ לִי, וּבְיָמַי אֶקְרָא. אֲפָפוּנִי חֶבְלֵי מָוֶת, וּמְצָרֵי שְׁאוֹל מְצָאוּנִי, צָרָה וְיָגוֹן אֶמְצָא. וּבְשֵׁם יְהֹוָה אֶקְרָא: אָנָּה יְהֹוָה, מַלְּטָה נַפְשִׁי. חַנּוּן יְהֹוָה וְצַדִּיק, וֵאלֹהֵינוּ מְרַחֵם. שֹׁמֵר פְּתָאיִם יְהֹוָה, דַּלּוֹתִי וְלִי יְהוֹשִׁיעַ. שׁוּבִי נַפְשִׁי לִמְנוּחָיְכִי, כִּי יְהֹוָה גָּמַל עָלָיְכִי. כִּי חִלַּצְתָּ נַפְשִׁי

rael. He will bless the House of Aharon; He will bless those who fear God, the small with the great. May God increase [blessing] upon you, upon you and upon your children. You are blessed to God, the Maker of Heaven and Earth. The Heavens are the heavens of God, but the Earth He gave to the children of man. The dead do not praise God, nor do those that go down to *Dumah*. But we will bless God, from now to eternity. Halleluyah!

I love God, because He hears my voice, my prayers. For He turned His ear to me. All my days I will call [upon Him]. The pangs of death encompassed me, and the agonies of the grave came upon me, trouble and sorrow I encounter and I call upon the Name of God. Please, God, deliver my soul! God is gra-

Hallel

cious and just, our God is compassionate. God watches over the simpletons; I was brought low and He saved me. Return, my soul, to your rest, for God has dealt kindly with you. For You have delivered my soul from death, my eyes from tears, my foot from stumbling. I will walk before God in the lands of the living. I had faith even when I said, "I am greatly afflicted." I said in my haste, "All men are deceitful."

What can I repay God for all His kindness to me? I will raise the cup of salvation and call upon the Name of God. I will pay my vows to God in the presence of all His people. Precious in the eyes of God is the death of His pious ones. I thank you, God, for I am Your servant. I am Your servant the son of Your handmaid. You have loosened my bonds. To You I will bring an offering of thanksgiving, and I will call upon the Name of God. I will pay my vows to God in the presence of all His peo-

מִמָּוֶת, אֶת עֵינִי מִן דִּמְעָה, אֶת רַגְלִי מִדֶּחִי. אֶתְהַלֵּךְ לִפְנֵי יְהֹוָה, בְּאַרְצוֹת הַחַיִּים. הֶאֱמַנְתִּי כִּי אֲדַבֵּר, אֲנִי עָנִיתִי מְאֹד. אֲנִי אָמַרְתִּי בְחָפְזִי: כָּל הָאָדָם כֹּזֵב.

מָה אָשִׁיב לַיהֹוָה, כָּל תַּגְמוּלוֹהִי עָלָי. כּוֹס יְשׁוּעוֹת אֶשָּׂא, וּבְשֵׁם יְהֹוָה אֶקְרָא. נְדָרַי לַיהֹוָה אֲשַׁלֵּם, נֶגְדָה נָּא לְכָל עַמּוֹ. יָקָר בְּעֵינֵי יְהֹוָה, הַמָּוְתָה לַחֲסִידָיו. אָנָּה יְהֹוָה כִּי אֲנִי עַבְדֶּךָ, אֲנִי עַבְדְּךָ בֶּן אֲמָתֶךָ, פִּתַּחְתָּ לְמוֹסֵרָי. לְךָ אֶזְבַּח זֶבַח תּוֹדָה, וּבְשֵׁם יְהֹוָה אֶקְרָא. נְדָרַי לַיהֹוָה אֲשַׁלֵּם, נֶגְדָה נָּא לְכָל עַמּוֹ. בְּחַצְרוֹת בֵּית יְהֹוָה, בְּתוֹכֵכִי יְרוּשָׁלָיִם. הַלְלוּיָהּ.

Hallel

ple, in the courtyards of the House of God, in the midst of Jerusalem. *Halleluyah*!

הַלְלוּ אֶת יְהוָה כָּל גּוֹיִם, שַׁבְּחוּהוּ כָּל הָאֻמִּים. כִּי גָבַר עָלֵינוּ חַסְדּוֹ, וֶאֱמֶת יְהוָה לְעוֹלָם. הַלְלוּיָהּ.

Praise God, all nations! Praise Him, all peoples! For His kindness was mighty over us, and the truth of God is everlasting. *Halleluyah*!

הוֹדוּ לַיהוָה כִּי טוֹב, כִּי לְעוֹלָם חַסְדּוֹ.

Give thanks to God, for He is good, for His kindness is everlasting.

יֹאמַר נָא יִשְׂרָאֵל, כִּי לְעוֹלָם חַסְדּוֹ.

Let Israel say [it], for His kindness is everlasting.

יֹאמְרוּ נָא בֵית אַהֲרֹן, כִּי לְעוֹלָם חַסְדּוֹ.

Let the House of Aharon say [it], for His kindness is everlasting.

יֹאמְרוּ נָא יִרְאֵי יְהוָה, כִּי לְעוֹלָם חַסְדּוֹ.

Let those who fear God say [it], for His kindness is everlasting.

מִן הַמֵּצַר קָרָאתִי יָּהּ, עָנָנִי בַמֶּרְחָב יָהּ. יְהוָה לִי לֹא אִירָא, מַה יַּעֲשֶׂה לִי אָדָם. יְהוָה לִי בְּעֹזְרָי, וַאֲנִי אֶרְאֶה בְשֹׂנְאָי. טוֹב לַחֲסוֹת בַּיהוָה, מִבְּטֹחַ בָּאָדָם. טוֹב לַחֲסוֹת בַּיהוָה,

Out of narrow straights I called to God, and God answered me with abounding relief. God is with me, I will not fear what man can do to me. God is with me, through my helpers, and I

Hallel

מִבְּטֹחַ בִּנְדִיבִים. כָּל גּוֹיִם סְבָבוּנִי, בְּשֵׁם יְהֹוָה כִּי אֲמִילַם. סַבּוּנִי גַם סְבָבוּנִי, בְּשֵׁם יְהֹוָה כִּי אֲמִילַם. סַבּוּנִי כִדְבוֹרִים דֹּעֲכוּ כְּאֵשׁ קוֹצִים, בְּשֵׁם יְהֹוָה כִּי אֲמִילַם. דָּחֹה דְחִיתַנִי לִנְפֹּל, וַיהֹוָה עֲזָרָנִי. עָזִּי וְזִמְרָת יָהּ, וַיְהִי לִי לִישׁוּעָה. קוֹל רִנָּה וִישׁוּעָה בְּאָהֳלֵי צַדִּיקִים, יְמִין יְהֹוָה עֹשָׂה חָיִל. יְמִין יְהֹוָה רוֹמֵמָה, יְמִין יְהֹוָה עֹשָׂה חָיִל. לֹא אָמוּת כִּי אֶחְיֶה, וַאֲסַפֵּר מַעֲשֵׂי יָהּ. יַסֹּר יִסְּרַנִּי יָּהּ, וְלַמָּוֶת לֹא נְתָנָנִי.

can face my enemies. It is better to rely on God, than to trust in man. It is better to rely on God, than to trust in nobles. All nations surround me, but I cut them down in the Name of God. They surrounded me, they encompassed me, but I cut them down in the Name of God. They surrounded me like bees, yet they are extinguished like a fire of thorns. I cut them down in the Name of God. You [my foes] pushed me again and again to fall, but God helped me. God is my strength and song, and this has been my salvation. The sound of joyous song and salvation is in the tents of the righteous: "The right hand of God performs deeds of valor. The right hand of God is exalted; the right hand of God performs deeds of valor!" I shall not die, but I shall live and relate the deeds of God. God has chastised me, but He did not give me over to death.

פִּתְחוּ לִי שַׁעֲרֵי צֶדֶק, אָבֹא בָם אוֹדֶה יָהּ. זֶה הַשַּׁעַר

Open for me the gates of righteousness; I will enter them and

Hallel

לַיהוָה, צַדִּיקִים יָבֹאוּ בוֹ. אוֹדְךָ כִּי עֲנִיתָנִי, וַתְּהִי לִי לִישׁוּעָה. אֶבֶן מָאֲסוּ הַבּוֹנִים, הָיְתָה לְרֹאשׁ פִּנָּה. מֵאֵת יְהוָה הָיְתָה זֹּאת, הִיא נִפְלָאת בְּעֵינֵינוּ. זֶה הַיּוֹם עָשָׂה יְהוָה, נָגִילָה וְנִשְׂמְחָה בוֹ.

אָנָּא יְהוָה הוֹשִׁיעָה נָּא, אָנָּא יְהוָה הַצְלִיחָה נָּא.

בָּרוּךְ הַבָּא בְּשֵׁם יְהוָה, בֵּרַכְנוּכֶם מִבֵּית יְהוָה. אֵל יְהוָה, וַיָּאֶר לָנוּ, אִסְרוּ חַג בַּעֲבֹתִים עַד קַרְנוֹת הַמִּזְבֵּחַ. אֵלִי אַתָּה וְאוֹדֶךָּ, אֱלֹהַי אֲרוֹמְמֶךָּ. הוֹדוּ לַיהוָה כִּי טוֹב, כִּי לְעוֹלָם חַסְדּוֹ.

יְהַלְלוּךָ יְיָ אֱלֹהֵינוּ כָּל מַעֲשֶׂיךָ, וַחֲסִידֶיךָ צַדִּיקִים עוֹשֵׂי רְצוֹנֶךָ, וְכָל עַמְּךָ בֵּית יִשְׂרָאֵל בְּרִנָּה יוֹדוּ וִיבָרְכוּ, וִישַׁבְּחוּ וִיפָאֲרוּ, וִירוֹמְמוּ וְיַעֲרִיצוּ, וְיַקְדִּישׁוּ

give thanks to God. This is the gate of God, the righteous will enter it. I thank You for You have answered me, and You have been a help to me. The stone scorned by the builders has become the main cornerstone. This was indeed from God, it is wondrous in our eyes. This day God has made, let us be glad and rejoice on it.

O God, please help us! O God, please help us! O God, please grant us success! O God, please grant us success!

Blessed is he who comes in the Name of God; we bless you from the House of God. God is Almighty, He gave us light; bind the festival-offering until [you bring it to] the horns of the altar. Give thanks to God, for He is good, for His kindness is everlasting.

God, our God, all Your works shall praise You. Your pious

Hallel

וְיַמְלִיכוּ אֶת שִׁמְךָ, מַלְכֵּנוּ. כִּי לְךָ טוֹב לְהוֹדוֹת וּלְשִׁמְךָ נָאֶה לְזַמֵּר, כִּי מֵעוֹלָם וְעַד עוֹלָם אַתָּה אֵל.

ones, the righteous who do Your will, and all Your people, the House of Israel, with joyous song will thank and bless, laud and glorify, exalt and adore, sanctify and proclaim the sovereignty of Your Name, our King. For it is good to thank You, and befitting to sing to Your Name, for from the beginning to the end of the world You are Almighty God.

THE HALLEL OF *Rosh Chodesh* and holidays does not usually include the following. But the night of the *Seder* is special, almost timeless. We have extra energy and are overflowing with gratitude to God, so why not take advantage and maximize the opportunity?

הוֹדוּ לַיהוָה כִּי טוֹב, כִּי לְעוֹלָם חַסְדּוֹ.

Give thanks to God, for He is good for His kindness is everlasting.

הוֹדוּ לֵאלֹהֵי הָאֱלֹהִים, כִּי לְעוֹלָם חַסְדּוֹ.

Give thanks to God of Gods, for His kindness is everlasting.

הוֹדוּ לַאֲדֹנֵי הָאֲדֹנִים, כִּי לְעֹלָם חַסְדּוֹ.

Give thanks to God of Gods, for His kindness is everlasting;

לְעֹשֵׂה נִפְלָאוֹת גְּדֹלוֹת לְבַדּוֹ,

Who alone does great wonders

Hallel

כִּי לְעוֹלָם חַסְדּוֹ.	for His kindness is everlasting.
לְעֹשֵׂה הַשָּׁמַיִם בִּתְבוּנָה, כִּי לְעוֹלָם חַסְדּוֹ.	Who made the heavens with understanding for His kindness is everlasting.
לְרֹקַע הָאָרֶץ עַל הַמָּיִם, כִּי לְעוֹלָם חַסְדּוֹ.	Who stretched out the earth above the waters for His kindness is everlasting.
לְעֹשֵׂה אוֹרִים גְּדֹלִים, כִּי לְעוֹלָם חַסְדּוֹ.	Who made the great lights for His kindness is everlasting.
אֶת הַשֶּׁמֶשׁ לְמֶמְשֶׁלֶת בַּיּוֹם, כִּי לְעוֹלָם חַסְדּוֹ.	The sun, to rule by day for His kindness is everlasting.
אֶת הַיָּרֵחַ וְכוֹכָבִים לְמֶמְשְׁלוֹת בַּלָּיְלָה, כִּי לְעוֹלָם חַסְדּוֹ.	The moon and stars, to rule by night for His kindness is everlasting.
לְמַכֵּה מִצְרַיִם בִּבְכוֹרֵיהֶם, כִּי לְעוֹלָם חַסְדּוֹ.	Who struck Egypt through their firstborn for His kindness is everlasting.
וַיּוֹצֵא יִשְׂרָאֵל מִתּוֹכָם, כִּי לְעוֹלָם חַסְדּוֹ.	And brought Israel out of their midst for His kindness is everlasting.
בְּיָד חֲזָקָה וּבִזְרוֹעַ נְטוּיָה, כִּי לְעוֹלָם חַסְדּוֹ.	With a strong hand and with an outstretched arm for His kindness is everlasting.
לְגֹזֵר יַם סוּף לִגְזָרִים, כִּי לְעוֹלָם חַסְדּוֹ.	

Hallel

וְהֶעֱבִיר יִשְׂרָאֵל בְּתוֹכוֹ, כִּי לְעוֹלָם חַסְדּוֹ.	Who split the Sea of Reeds into sections for His kindness is everlasting.
וְנִעֵר פַּרְעֹה וְחֵילוֹ בְיַם סוּף, כִּי לְעוֹלָם חַסְדּוֹ.	And led Israel through it for His kindness is everlasting.
לְמוֹלִיךְ עַמּוֹ בַּמִּדְבָּר, כִּי לְעוֹלָם חַסְדּוֹ.	And cast Pharaoh and his army into the Sea of Reeds for His kindness is everlasting.
לְמַכֵּה מְלָכִים גְּדֹלִים, כִּי לְעוֹלָם חַסְדּוֹ.	Who led His people through the desert for His kindness is everlasting.
וַיַּהֲרֹג מְלָכִים אַדִּירִים, כִּי לְעוֹלָם חַסְדּוֹ.	Who struck great kings for His kindness is everlasting.
לְסִיחוֹן מֶלֶךְ הָאֱמֹרִי, כִּי לְעוֹלָם חַסְדּוֹ.	And slew mighty kings for His kindness is everlasting.
וּלְעוֹג מֶלֶךְ הַבָּשָׁן, כִּי לְעוֹלָם חַסְדּוֹ.	Sichon, king of the Amorites for His kindness is everlasting.
וְנָתַן אַרְצָם לְנַחֲלָה, כִּי לְעוֹלָם חַסְדּוֹ.	And Og, king of Bashan for His kindness is everlasting.
נַחֲלָה לְיִשְׂרָאֵל עַבְדּוֹ, כִּי לְעוֹלָם חַסְדּוֹ.	And gave their land as a heritage for His kindness is everlasting.
שֶׁבְּשִׁפְלֵנוּ זָכַר לָנוּ, כִּי לְעוֹלָם	A heritage to Israel, His servant

Hallel

חַסְדוֹ.	for His kindness is everlasting.
וַיִּפְרְקֵנוּ מִצָּרֵינוּ, כִּי לְעוֹלָם חַסְדוֹ.	Who remembered us in our lowliness for His kindness is everlasting.
נֹתֵן לֶחֶם לְכָל בָּשָׂר, כִּי לְעוֹלָם חַסְדוֹ.	And delivered us from our oppressors for His kindness is everlasting.
הוֹדוּ לְאֵל הַשָּׁמָיִם, כִּי לְעוֹלָם חַסְדוֹ.	Who gives food to all flesh for His kindness is everlasting.

Thank the God of heaven for His kindness is everlasting.

We have already praised God *a lot*, but is it ever enough? It depends. If the praise is for God, then yes, because He doesn't *need* our praise. He doesn't need *anything* from us. He is perfect already, and certainly does not need our praise to feel better about Himself, or at all.

Then who do we do it for? For ourselves. When it comes to human beings, both sides benefit from the praise of another. But when it comes to God, we are the sole beneficiaries—or rather, *soul* beneficiaries—of our praise. And not just because it feels good to acknowledge the help of another, but because it is the best way to enhance our connection to God, and feel more alive because of it.

There is a story of a father who wanted to teach his teenage son the value of money. The young man was earning his own money, but spending it as fast he made it. So the father told his son that it was time he helped out at home by contributing some of his money.

The child was shocked and angry at first but complied, and after a while, the son just got used to the "tax." He had no idea that the father wasn't actually spending the money, but secretly saving it for the son's future when he would need and want it the most.

Years passed and the son was engaged to get married. At the *chasunah*, the father handed his son a thick envelope, who asked, "What's this?" The father smiled and said, "It's all the money you thought you were paying over the years to earn your keep. In fact, I was saving it for this day so you would have it to start off your new life together…"

The son looked inside the envelope and was suddenly overwhelmed with emotion. Not only had his father acted wisely when he hadn't, but he had given him a head start on his new life with thousands of dollars saved up over the years. As the son cried with appreciation he told his father, "If I had known that is why you wanted the money, I would have given you more!"

Likewise, when we later find out how God put away each

Hallel

word of praise we spoke in a special "envelope" for the World to Come, we'll wish we had done more of it when we could have:

We learn from this that the light of the *Shechinah*, for those who merit to see it, is the splendor and pleasantness of all life in the World to Come. This is what it [means when it] says, *"All the actions of God are for His sake,"* that is, for the sake of [the revelation of] His light to be revealed to those who are worthy of this. (*Chelek HaBiurim, Drushei Igulim v'Yoshar, Anaf* 1, *Os* 1)

When we praise God, *we do this*. The more we praise Him, the more we fulfill the purpose of Creation, and our purpose as well.

נִשְׁמַת כָּל חַי תְּבָרֵךְ אֶת שִׁמְךָ, יְיָ אֱלֹהֵינוּ, וְרוּחַ כָּל בָּשָׂר תְּפָאֵר וּתְרוֹמֵם זִכְרְךָ, מַלְכֵּנוּ, תָּמִיד. מִן הָעוֹלָם וְעַד הָעוֹלָם אַתָּה אֵל, וּמִבַּלְעָדֶיךָ אֵין לָנוּ מֶלֶךְ גּוֹאֵל וּמוֹשִׁיעַ, פּוֹדֶה וּמַצִּיל וּמְפַרְנֵס וּמְרַחֵם בְּכָל עֵת צָרָה וְצוּקָה. אֵין לָנוּ מֶלֶךְ אֶלָּא אַתָּה. אֱלֹהֵי הָרִאשׁוֹנִים	The soul of every living being shall bless Your Name, God, our God, and the spirit of all flesh shall always glorify and exalt Your remembrance, our King. From the beginning to the end of the world You are Almighty God, and other than You we have no King, Redeemer and Savior who delivers, rescues, sustains, answers

Hallel

וְהָאַחֲרוֹנִים, אֱלוֹהַּ כָּל בְּרִיּוֹת, אֲדוֹן כָּל תּוֹלָדוֹת הַמְהֻלָּל בְּרֹב הַתִּשְׁבָּחוֹת, הַמְנַהֵג עוֹלָמוֹ בְּחֶסֶד וּבְרִיּוֹתָיו בְּרַחֲמִים. וַיְיָ לֹא יָנוּם וְלֹא יִישָׁן הַמְעוֹרֵר יְשֵׁנִים וְהַמֵּקִיץ נִרְדָּמִים, וְהַמֵּשִׂיחַ אִלְּמִים וְהַמַּתִּיר אֲסוּרִים, וְהַסּוֹמֵךְ נוֹפְלִים וְהַזּוֹקֵף כְּפוּפִים. לְךָ לְבַדְּךָ אֲנַחְנוּ מוֹדִים. (וְ)אִלּוּ פִינוּ מָלֵא שִׁירָה כַּיָּם, וּלְשׁוֹנֵנוּ רִנָּה כַּהֲמוֹן גַּלָּיו, וְשִׂפְתוֹתֵינוּ שֶׁבַח כְּמֶרְחֲבֵי רָקִיעַ, וְעֵינֵינוּ מְאִירוֹת כַּשֶּׁמֶשׁ וְכַיָּרֵחַ, וְיָדֵינוּ פְרוּשׂוֹת כְּנִשְׁרֵי שָׁמַיִם, וְרַגְלֵינוּ קַלּוֹת כָּאַיָּלוֹת אֵין אֲנַחְנוּ מַסְפִּיקִים לְהוֹדוֹת לְךָ, יְיָ אֱלֹהֵינוּ וֵאלֹהֵי אֲבוֹתֵינוּ, וּלְבָרֵךְ אֶת שְׁמֶךָ, עַל אַחַת מֵאֶלֶף אַלְפֵי אֲלָפִים וְרִבֵּי רְבָבוֹת פְּעָמִים, הַטּוֹבוֹת שֶׁעָשִׂיתָ עִם אֲבוֹתֵינוּ וְעִמָּנוּ: מִמִּצְרַיִם

and is merciful in every time of trouble and distress; we have no King but You. [You are] the God of the first and of the last [generations], God of all creatures, God of all events, who is praised with manifold praises, who directs His world with kindness and His creatures with compassion. God neither slumbers nor sleeps. He arouses the sleepers and awakens the slumberous, gives speech to the mute, releases the bound, supports the falling and raises up those who are bowed. To You alone we give thanks. Even if our mouths were filled with song as the sea, and our tongues with joyous singing like the multitudes of its waves, and our lips with praise like the expanse of the sky; and our eyes shining like the sun and the moon, and our hands spread out like the eagles of heaven, and our feet

Hallel

גְּאַלְתָּנוּ יְיָ אֱלֹהֵינוּ, וּמִבֵּית עֲבָדִים פְּדִיתָנוּ, בְּרָעָב זַנְתָּנוּ וּבְשָׂבָע כִּלְכַּלְתָּנוּ, מֵחֶרֶב הִצַּלְתָּנוּ וּמִדֶּבֶר מִלַּטְתָּנוּ, וּמֵחֳלָיִם רָעִים וְנֶאֱמָנִים דִּלִּיתָנוּ. עַד הֵנָּה עֲזָרוּנוּ רַחֲמֶיךָ וְלֹא עֲזָבוּנוּ חֲסָדֶיךָ, וְאַל תִּטְּשֵׁנוּ, יְיָ אֱלֹהֵינוּ, לָנֶצַח. עַל כֵּן אֵבָרִים שֶׁפִּלַּגְתָּ בָּנוּ, וְרוּחַ וּנְשָׁמָה שֶׁנָּפַחְתָּ בְּאַפֵּינוּ, וְלָשׁוֹן אֲשֶׁר שַׂמְתָּ בְּפִינוּ הֵן הֵם יוֹדוּ וִיבָרְכוּ וִישַׁבְּחוּ וִיפָאֲרוּ וִירוֹמְמוּ וְיַעֲרִיצוּ וְיַקְדִּישׁוּ וְיַמְלִיכוּ אֶת שִׁמְךָ מַלְכֵּנוּ. כִּי כָל פֶּה לְךָ יוֹדֶה, וְכָל לָשׁוֹן לְךָ תִּשָּׁבַע, וְכָל בֶּרֶךְ לְךָ תִכְרַע, וְכָל קוֹמָה לְפָנֶיךָ תִשְׁתַּחֲוֶה, וְכָל לְבָבוֹת יִירָאוּךָ, וְכָל קֶרֶב וּכְלָיוֹת יְזַמְּרוּ לִשְׁמֶךָ, כַּדָּבָר שֶׁכָּתוּב: "כָּל עַצְמֹתַי תֹּאמַרְנָה: יְיָ, מִי כָמוֹךָ מַצִּיל עָנִי מֵחָזָק מִמֶּנּוּ, וְעָנִי וְאֶבְיוֹן מִגֹּזְלוֹ" (תהלים לה:י). מִי

swift like deer we would still be unable to thank You God, our God and God of our fathers, and to bless Your Name, for even one of the thousands of millions, and myriads of myriads, of favors, miracles and wonders which You have done for us and for our fathers before us. God, our God. You have redeemed us from Egypt, You have freed us from the house of bondage, You have fed us in famine and nourished us in plenty; You have saved us from the sword and delivered us from pestilence, and raised us from evil and lasting illnesses. Until now Your mercies have helped us, and Your kindnesses have not abandoned us; and do not desert us, God our God, forever! Therefore, the limbs which You have arranged within us, and the spirit and soul which You have breathed into

Hallel

יִדְמֶה לָּךְ וּמִי יִשְׁוֶה לָּךְ וּמִי יַעֲרָךְ לָךְ הָאֵל הַגָּדוֹל, הַגִּבּוֹר וְהַנּוֹרָא, אֵל עֶלְיוֹן, קֹנֵה שָׁמַיִם וָאָרֶץ. נְהַלֶּלְךָ וּנְשַׁבֵּחֲךָ וּנְפָאֶרְךָ וּנְבָרֵךְ אֶת שֵׁם קָדְשֶׁךָ, כָּאָמוּר: "לְדָוִד בָּרְכִי נַפְשִׁי אֶת יְיָ, וְכָל קְרָבַי אֶת שֵׁם קָדְשׁוֹ".

הָאֵל בְּתַעֲצֻמוֹת עֻזֶּךָ, הַגָּדוֹל בִּכְבוֹד שְׁמֶךָ, הַגִּבּוֹר לָנֶצַח וְהַנּוֹרָא בְּנוֹרְאוֹתֶיךָ, הַמֶּלֶךְ הַיּוֹשֵׁב עַל כִּסֵּא רָם וְנִשָּׂא.

שׁוֹכֵן עַד מָרוֹם וְקָדוֹשׁ שְׁמוֹ. וְכָתוּב: "רַנְּנוּ צַדִּיקִים בַּיהוָה לַיְשָׁרִים נָאוָה תְהִלָּה" (תהלים לג:א). בְּפִי יְשָׁרִים תִּתְהַלָּל, וּבְדִבְרֵי צַדִּיקִים תִּתְבָּרַךְ, וּבִלְשׁוֹן חֲסִידִים תִּתְרוֹמָם, וּבְקֶרֶב קְדוֹשִׁים תִּתְקַדָּשׁ.

וּבְמַקְהֲלוֹת רִבְבוֹת עַמְּךָ בֵּית יִשְׂרָאֵל בְּרִנָּה יִתְפָּאֵר שִׁמְךָ, מַלְכֵּנוּ, בְּכָל דּוֹר וָדוֹר, שֶׁכֵּן

our nostrils, and the tongue which You have placed in our mouth they all shall thank, bless, praise, glorify, exalt, adore, sanctify and proclaim the sovereignty of Your Name, our King. For every mouth shall offer thanks to You, every tongue shall swear by You, every eye shall look to You, every knee shall bend to You, all who stand erect shall bow down before You, all hearts shall fear You, and every innermost part shall sing praise to Your Name, as it says: *"All my bones will say, God, who is like You; You save the poor from one stronger than he, the poor and the needy from one who would rob him!"* Who can be likened to You, who is equal to You, who can be compared to You, the great, mighty, awesome God, God most high, Possessor of heaven and earth! We will laud You,

143

Hallel

חוֹבַת כָּל הַיְצוּרִים לְפָנֶיךָ, יְיָ אֱלֹהֵינוּ וֵאלֹהֵי אֲבוֹתֵינוּ, לְהוֹדוֹת, לְהַלֵּל, לְשַׁבֵּחַ, לְפָאֵר, לְרוֹמֵם, לְהַדֵּר, לְנַצֵּחַ, לְבָרֵךְ, לְעַלֵּה וּלְקַלֵּס, עַל כָּל דִּבְרֵי שִׁירוֹת וְתִשְׁבָּחוֹת דָּוִד בֶּן יִשַׁי עַבְדְּךָ, מְשִׁיחֶךָ.

יִשְׁתַּבַּח שִׁמְךָ לָעַד מַלְכֵּנוּ, הָאֵל הַמֶּלֶךְ הַגָּדוֹל וְהַקָּדוֹשׁ בַּשָּׁמַיִם וּבָאָרֶץ, כִּי לְךָ נָאֶה, יְיָ אֱלֹהֵינוּ וֵאלֹהֵי אֲבוֹתֵינוּ, שִׁיר וּשְׁבָחָה, הַלֵּל וְזִמְרָה, עֹז וּמֶמְשָׁלָה, נֶצַח, גְּדֻלָּה וּגְבוּרָה, תְּהִלָּה וְתִפְאֶרֶת קְדֻשָּׁה וּמַלְכוּת, בְּרָכוֹת וְהוֹדָאוֹת מֵעַתָּה וְעַד עוֹלָם. בָּרוּךְ אַתָּה יְיָ, אֵל מֶלֶךְ גָּדוֹל בַּתִּשְׁבָּחוֹת, אֵל הַהוֹדָאוֹת, אֲדוֹן הַנִּפְלָאוֹת, הַבּוֹחֵר בְּשִׁירֵי זִמְרָה, מֶלֶךְ אֵל חֵי הָעוֹלָמִים.

praise You and glorify You, and we will bless Your holy Name, as it says: *"By Dovid; bless God, O my soul, and all that is within me [bless] His holy Name."* You are the Almighty God in the power of Your strength; the Great in the glory of Your Name; the Mighty forever, and the Awesome in Your awesome deeds; the King who sits upon a lofty and exalted throne. He who dwells for eternity, lofty and holy is His Name. And it is written: *"Sing joyously to God, you righteous; it befits the upright to offer praise."* By the mouth of the upright You are exalted; by the lips of the righteous You are blessed ; by the tongue of the pious You are sanctified; and among the holy ones You are praised.

In the assemblies of the myriads of Your people, the House of Israel, Your Name, our King, shall be glorified with song in every generation. For such is the obligation of all creatures before You, God, our God and God of our fathers, to thank, to laud, to praise, to glorify, to exalt, to adore, to bless, to elevate and to honor You, even beyond all the words of songs and praises of Dovid son of Yishai, Your anointed servant.

May Your Name be praised forever, our King, the great and holy God and King in heaven and on earth. For You it is fitting, God, our God and God of our fathers, song and praise, praise and song, strength and rulership, victory, greatness and might, glory, splendor, holiness and sovereignty; blessings and thanksgivings from now and forever. Blessed are You, God, Almighty King, great in praises, Almighty of thanks, Master of wonders, Who chooses songs, King, Almighty life of all worlds.

The Fourth Cup

IT IS NOW time to conclude the *Seder* with the fourth and final cup of wine which corresponds to, *"And I will take you —velakachti—to Me as a people."* This itself is reason to pause and consider the implications, because it is this that changed the destiny of the descendants of Avraham, and of the world for that matter.

God did not make Creation for His amusement. We're not that amusing. He made it for one reason and one reason only, and that is to give something created the opportunity

Hallel

to know and relate to Him.[2] It was not for His benefit because, as pointed out earlier, God lacks nothing which means that there is nothing we can give Him that He didn't already have, having everything already.

That shows how fundamentally good God is. He gives good but, unlike humans, derives no personal benefit from doing so. And though every human is clearly able to have a relationship with God, it is Torah that provides the means to have the closest relationship with God possible. This leads to incredible pleasure in this world and unimaginable pleasure in the next world, all of which is a function of *"velakachti,"* something to consider while drinking the fourth cup of wine.

As with respect to the previous three cups, a person should drink at least the majority of the cup, and reclining to the left. The blessing for the wine is said first:

בָּרוּךְ אַתָּה יְיָ אֱלֹהֵינוּ מֶלֶךְ הָעוֹלָם, בּוֹרֵא פְּרִי הַגָּפֶן.   Blessed are You, God, our God, King of the universe, who creates the fruit of the vine.

After drinking the wine, this Brochah Acharonah for wine is immediately said:

---

[2] *Derech Hashem*, Purpose of Creation.

Hallel

בָּרוּךְ אַתָּה יְיָ אֱלֹהֵינוּ מֶלֶךְ הָעוֹלָם, עַל הַגֶּפֶן וְעַל פְּרִי הַגֶּפֶן, עַל תְּנוּבַת הַשָּׂדֶה וְעַל אֶרֶץ חֶמְדָּה טוֹבָה וּרְחָבָה שֶׁרָצִיתָ וְהִנְחַלְתָּ לַאֲבוֹתֵינוּ לֶאֱכֹל מִפִּרְיָהּ וְלִשְׂבֹּעַ מִטּוּבָהּ. רַחֵם נָא יְיָ אֱלֹהֵינוּ עַל יִשְׂרָאֵל עַמֶּךָ וְעַל יְרוּשָׁלַיִם עִירֶךָ וְעַל צִיּוֹן מִשְׁכַּן כְּבוֹדֶךָ וְעַל מִזְבְּחֶךָ וְעַל הֵיכָלֶךָ. וּבְנֵה יְרוּשָׁלַיִם עִיר הַקֹּדֶשׁ בִּמְהֵרָה בְיָמֵינוּ, וְהַעֲלֵנוּ לְתוֹכָהּ וְשַׂמְּחֵנוּ בְּבִנְיָנָהּ וְנֹאכַל מִפִּרְיָהּ וְנִשְׂבַּע מִטּוּבָהּ וּנְבָרֶכְךָ עָלֶיהָ בִּקְדֻשָּׁה וּבְטָהֳרָה (בְּשַׁבָּת: וּרְצֵה וְהַחֲלִיצֵנוּ בְּיוֹם הַשַּׁבָּת הַזֶּה) וְשַׂמְּחֵנוּ בְּיוֹם חַג הַמַּצּוֹת הַזֶּה, כִּי אַתָּה יְיָ טוֹב וּמֵטִיב לַכֹּל וְנוֹדֶה לְךָ עַל הָאָרֶץ וְעַל פְּרִי הַגֶּפֶן. בָּרוּךְ אַתָּה יְיָ עַל הָאָרֶץ וְעַל פְּרִי הַגֶּפֶן (בא״י: וְעַל פְּרִי גַפְנָהּ).

Blessed are You, God our God, King of the universe for the vine and the fruit of the vine, for the produce of the field, and for the precious, good and spacious land which You have favored to give as a heritage to our fathers, to eat of its fruit and be satiated by its goodness. Have mercy, God our God, on Israel Your people, on Jerusalem Your city, on Zion the abode of Your glory, on Your altar and on Your Temple. Rebuild Jerusalem, the holy city, speedily in our days, and bring us up into it, and make us rejoice in it, and we will bless You in holiness and purity (*Shabbos*: May it please You to strengthen us on this *Shabbos* day) and remember us for good on this day of the Festival of *Matzos*. For You, God, are good and do good to all, and we thank You for the land and

Hallel

for the fruit of the vine. Blessed are You, God, for the land and for the fruit of the vine.

The word *hallel*—praise—also means *light* (*Pesachim* 2a). It has a *gematria* of 5+30+30, or 65, the same total *gematria* as God's Name, *Adonai* (1+4+50+10), which corresponds to the level of Malchus and of our reality. When we say *Hallel*, especially with the proper intention, we draw down the light of God into our world, causing rectification

Nirtzah

נרצה

IT IS HOURS since the *Seder* began. Other than on *Yom Kippur*, we do not do so much to help us get into the spirit of the occasion, even on *Rosh Hashanah*, the Day of Judgment. *Seder Night* is probably the most special night of the Jewish year.

Even more interesting is that it is also the only night that we do not need to do something to access the light. Normally, the activities of a holiday are designed to give us access to the special light that emanates on a particular holiday. On the night of the *Seder*, the light emanates on its own, just as it did the night of the first *Seder*, back in Egypt.

So why all the different parts of the *Seder*? Just to make sure that when the light comes down, we're in the right place, physical and spiritually, to receive it. It is possible that when the opportunity of *Pesach* comes knocking that we will be distracted doing something else.[1] The *Seder* is designed to make sure that we're ready to receive the gift of the light of freedom meant for us that night.

Hence, *Nirtzah*. We don't do anything like it on any other holiday. We're saying that we have done what was expected of us and hope that it was acceptable (*nirtzah*) to God. In the end, that is all that really concerns us, that what we do throughout the course of lives makes God pleased that He gave us life.

It is enough for many people to just be *yotzei*. They are satisfied knowing that they have done at least the minimal *mitzvah*, having thereby discharged their obligation. They don't see any value in putting more into a *mitzvah* because they think they will lose more by doing so than they will gain.

It's the oldest *yetzer hara* trick in the book, and if a person falls prey to it, then it means they are a slave to it. *Pesach* is *Zman Cheiraseinu*, the time for us to achieve freedom, physical if necessary but spiritual always. Going the extra distance to do a *mitzvah* that God can be proud of is a great way to measure that, and to become master of your own "home."

---

[1] *Hakdamas uSha'arim, Sha'ar* 6, Ch.. 6-7.

Nirtzah

חֲסַל סִדּוּר פֶּסַח כְּהִלְכָתוֹ, כְּכָל מִשְׁפָּטוֹ וְחֻקָּתוֹ.

כַּאֲשֶׁר זָכִינוּ לְסַדֵּר אוֹתוֹ, כֵּן נִזְכֶּה לַעֲשׂוֹתוֹ.

זָךְ שׁוֹכֵן מְעוֹנָה, קוֹמֵם קְהַל עֲדַת מִי מָנָה.

קָרֵב נַהֵל נִטְעֵי כַנָּה, פְּדוּיִם לְצִיּוֹן בְּרִנָּה.

The *Pesach* service is finished, as it was meant to be performed, in accordance with all its rules and laws.

Just as we have been privileged to lay out its order, so may we be privileged to perform it.

Pure One, dwelling in Your heaven, raise up this people, too abundant to be counted.

Soon, lead the shoots of stock, redeemed, into *Tzion* with great joy.

לְשָׁנָה הַבָּאָה בִּירוּשָׁלַיִם הַבְּנוּיָה.

Next year in re-built Jerusalem.

151

זְמִירוֹת

EVERYONE LOVES TO sing. But there are basically two types of songs, those that sing to the body and those that sing to the soul. Songs that sing to the body inspire, but not always to do the most meaningful things. But songs that sing to the soul—*zemiros*—inspire a person to be more Godly and, as a result, enhance their connection to God.

Those who contributed to the final version of the *Haggadah* did not add *zemiros* at the end of the *Seder* because they thought we might have some "leftover" time. They knew we'd be tired and, physically, ready to call it a night. But they also knew that anyone who completed the *Seder* as it was meant to be performed had freed their soul by the end, and that it would be a waste of opportunity to not let the soul sing.

וּבְכֵן וַיְהִי בַּחֲצִי הַלַּיְלָה

אָז רוֹב נִסִּים הִפְלֵאתָ בַּלַּיְלָה.
בְּרֹאשׁ אַשְׁמוֹרֶת זֶה הַלַּיְלָה.
גֵּר צֶדֶק נִצַּחְתּוֹ כְּנֶחֱלַק לוֹ לַיְלָה.
וַיְהִי בַּחֲצִי הַלַּיְלָה.

דַּנְתָּ מֶלֶךְ גְּרָר בַּחֲלוֹם הַלַּיְלָה.
הִפְחַדְתָּ אֲרַמִּי בְּאֶמֶשׁ לַיְלָה.
וַיָּשַׂר יִשְׂרָאֵל לְמַלְאָךְ וַיּוּכַל לוֹ לַיְלָה.
וַיְהִי בַּחֲצִי הַלַּיְלָה.

זֶרַע בְּכוֹרֵי פַתְרוֹס מָחַצְתָּ בַּחֲצִי הַלַּיְלָה.
חֵילָם לֹא מָצְאוּ בְּקוּמָם בַּלַּיְלָה.
טִיסַת נְגִיד חֲרֹשֶׁת סִלִּיתָ בְּכוֹכְבֵי לַיְלָה.
וַיְהִי בַּחֲצִי הַלַּיְלָה.

יָעַץ מְחָרֵף לְנוֹפֵף אִוּוּי, הוֹבַשְׁתָּ פְגָרָיו בַּלַּיְלָה.
כָּרַע בֵּל וּמַצָּבוֹ בְּאִישׁוֹן לַיְלָה.
לְאִישׁ חֲמוּדוֹת נִגְלָה רָז חֲזוֹת לַיְלָה, לַיְלָה.
וַיְהִי בַּחֲצִי הַלַּיְלָה.

Zemiros

מִשְׁתַּכֵּר בִּכְלֵי קֹדֶשׁ נֶהֱרַג בּוֹ בַּלַּיְלָה.
נוֹשַׁע מִבּוֹר אֲרָיוֹת פּוֹתֵר בִּעֲתוּתֵי לַיְלָה.
שִׂנְאָה נָטַר אֲגָגִי וְכָתַב סְפָרִים בַּלַּיְלָה.
וַיְהִי בַּחֲצִי הַלַּיְלָה.

עוֹרַרְתָּ נִצְחֲךָ עָלָיו בְּנֶדֶד שְׁנַת לַיְלָה.
פּוּרָה תִדְרוֹךְ לְשׁוֹמֵר מַה מִלַּיְלָה.
צָרַח כַּשּׁוֹמֵר וְשָׂח אָתָא בֹקֶר וְגַם לַיְלָה.
וַיְהִי בַּחֲצִי הַלַּיְלָה.

קָרֵב יוֹם אֲשֶׁר הוּא לֹא יוֹם וְלֹא לַיְלָה.
רָם הוֹדַע כִּי לְךָ הַיּוֹם אַף לְךָ הַלַּיְלָה.
שׁוֹמְרִים הַפְקֵד לְעִירְךָ כָּל הַיּוֹם וְכָל הַלַּיְלָה.
תָּאִיר כְּאוֹר יוֹם חֶשְׁכַת הַלַּיְלָה.
וַיְהִי בַּחֲצִי הַלַּיְלָה.

In Israel this is said at the first Seder, but outside of Israel it is said on the second night.

וּבְכֵן, וַאֲמַרְתֶּם זֶבַח פֶּסַח

אֹמֶץ גְּבוּרוֹתֶיךָ הִפְלֵאתָ בַּפֶּסַח.
בְּרֹאשׁ כָּל מוֹעֲדוֹת נִשֵּׂאתָ פֶּסַח.

154

Zemiros

גָּלִיתָ לְאֶזְרָחִי חֲצוֹת לֵיל   פֶּסַח.
וַאֲמַרְתֶּם זֶבַח פֶּסַח.

דְּלָתָיו דָּפַקְתָּ כְּחֹם הַיּוֹם   בַּפֶּסַח.
הִסְעִיד נוֹצְצִים עֻגוֹת מַצּוֹת   בַּפֶּסַח.
"וְאֶל הַבָּקָר רָץ" זֵכֶר לְשׁוֹר עֵרֶךְ   פֶּסַח.
וַאֲמַרְתֶּם זֶבַח פֶּסַח.

זוֹעֲמוּ סְדוֹמִים וְלוֹהֲטוּ בָּאֵשׁ   בַּפֶּסַח.
חֻלַּץ לוֹט מֵהֶם וּמַצּוֹת אָפָה בְּקֵץ   פֶּסַח.
טִאטֵאתָ אַדְמַת מֹף וְנֹף בְּעָבְרְךָ   בַּפֶּסַח.
וַאֲמַרְתֶּם זֶבַח פֶּסַח.

יָהּ, רֹאשׁ כָּל אוֹן מָחַצְתָּ בְּלֵיל שִׁמּוּר   פֶּסַח.
כַּבִּיר, עַל בֵּן בְּכוֹר פָּסַחְתָּ בְּדַם   פֶּסַח.
לְבִלְתִּי תֵּת מַשְׁחִית לָבֹא בִּפְתָחַי   בַּפֶּסַח.
וַאֲמַרְתֶּם זֶבַח פֶּסַח.

מְסֻגֶּרֶת סֻגָּרָה בְּעִתּוֹתֵי,   פֶּסַח.
נִשְׁמְדָה מִדְיָן בִּצְלִיל שְׂעוֹרֵי עֹמֶר   פֶּסַח.
שׂוֹרְפוּ מִשְׁמַנֵּי פּוּל וְלוּד בִּיקַד יְקוֹד   פֶּסַח.
וַאֲמַרְתֶּם זֶבַח פֶּסַח.

"עוֹד הַיּוֹם בְּנֹב לַעֲמוֹד עַד גְּעָה עוֹנַת פֶּסַח.
פַּס יָד כָּתְבָה לְקַעֲקֵעַ צוּל בַּפֶּסַח.
צָפֹה הַצָּפִית עָרוֹךְ הַשֻּׁלְחָן בַּפֶּסַח.
וַאֲמַרְתֶּם זֶבַח פֶּסַח.

קָהָל כִּנְּסָה הֲדַסָּה לְשַׁלֵּשׁ צוֹם בַּפֶּסַח.
רֹאשׁ מִבֵּית רָשָׁע מָחַצְתָּ בְּעֵץ חֲמִשִּׁים בַּפֶּסַח.
שְׁתֵּי אֵלֶּה רֶגַע תָּבִיא לְעוּצִית בַּפֶּסַח.
תָּעֹז יָדְךָ וְתָרוּם יְמִינְךָ כְּלֵיל הִתְקַדֶּשׁ חַג פֶּסַח.
וַאֲמַרְתֶּם זֶבַח פֶּסַח.

On both nights continue here:

כִּי לוֹ נָאֶה, כִּי לוֹ יָאֶה

אַדִּיר בִּמְלוּכָה, בָּחוּר כַּהֲלָכָה, גְּדוּדָיו יֹאמְרוּ לוֹ: לְךָ וּלְךָ, לְךָ כִּי לְךָ, לְךָ אַף לְךָ, לְךָ יְיָ הַמַּמְלָכָה, כִּי לוֹ נָאֶה, כִּי לוֹ יָאֶה.

דָּגוּל בִּמְלוּכָה, הָדוּר כַּהֲלָכָה, וָתִיקָיו יֹאמְרוּ לוֹ: לְךָ וּלְךָ, לְךָ כִּי לְךָ, לְךָ אַף לְךָ, לְךָ יְיָ הַמַּמְלָכָה, כִּי לוֹ נָאֶה, כִּי לוֹ יָאֶה.

זַכַּאי בִּמְלוּכָה, חָסִין כַּהֲלָכָה, טַפְסְרָיו יֹאמְרוּ
לוֹ: לְךָ וּלְךָ, לְךָ כִּי לְךָ, לְךָ אַף לְךָ, לְךָ יְיָ הַמַּמְלָכָה,
כִּי לוֹ נָאֶה, כִּי לוֹ יָאֶה.

יָחִיד בִּמְלוּכָה, כַּבִּיר כַּהֲלָכָה, לִמּוּדָיו יֹאמְרוּ
לוֹ: לְךָ וּלְךָ, לְךָ כִּי לְךָ, לְךָ אַף לְךָ, לְךָ יְיָ הַמַּמְלָכָה,
כִּי לוֹ נָאֶה, כִּי לוֹ יָאֶה.

מוֹשֵׁל בִּמְלוּכָה, נוֹרָא כַּהֲלָכָה, סְבִיבָיו יֹאמְרוּ
לוֹ: לְךָ וּלְךָ, לְךָ כִּי לְךָ, לְךָ אַף לְךָ, לְךָ יְיָ הַמַּמְלָכָה,
כִּי לוֹ נָאֶה, כִּי לוֹ יָאֶה.

עָנָיו בִּמְלוּכָה, פּוֹדֶה כַּהֲלָכָה, צַדִּיקָיו יֹאמְרוּ לוֹ:
לְךָ וּלְךָ, לְךָ כִּי לְךָ, לְךָ אַף לְךָ, לְךָ יְיָ הַמַּמְלָכָה,
כִּי לוֹ נָאֶה, כִּי לוֹ יָאֶה.

קָדוֹשׁ בִּמְלוּכָה, רַחוּם כַּהֲלָכָה, שִׁנְאַנָּיו יֹאמְרוּ
לוֹ: לְךָ וּלְךָ, לְךָ כִּי לְךָ, לְךָ אַף לְךָ, לְךָ יְיָ הַמַּמְלָכָה,
כִּי לוֹ נָאֶה, כִּי לוֹ יָאֶה.

תַּקִּיף בִּמְלוּכָה, תּוֹמֵךְ כַּהֲלָכָה, תְּמִימָיו יֹאמְרוּ
לוֹ: לְךָ וּלְךָ, לְךָ כִּי לְךָ, לְךָ אַף לְךָ, לְךָ יְיָ הַמַּמְלָכָה,
כִּי לוֹ נָאֶה, כִּי לוֹ יָאֶה.

אַדִּיר הוּא יִבְנֶה בֵּיתוֹ

אַדִּיר הוּא יִבְנֶה בֵּיתוֹ בְּקָרוֹב. בִּמְהֵרָה, בִּמְהֵרָה, בְּיָמֵינוּ בְּקָרוֹב. אֵל בְּנֵה, אֵל בְּנֵה, בְּנֵה בֵּיתְךָ בְּקָרוֹב.

בָּחוּר הוּא, גָּדוֹל הוּא, דָּגוּל הוּא יִבְנֶה בֵּיתוֹ בְּקָרוֹב. בִּמְהֵרָה, בִּמְהֵרָה, בְּיָמֵינוּ בְּקָרוֹב. אֵל בְּנֵה, אֵל בְּנֵה, בְּנֵה בֵּיתְךָ בְּקָרוֹב.

הָדוּר הוּא, וָתִיק הוּא, זַכַּאי הוּא, חָסִיד הוּא יִבְנֶה בֵּיתוֹ בְּקָרוֹב. בִּמְהֵרָה, בִּמְהֵרָה, בְּיָמֵינוּ בְּקָרוֹב. אֵל בְּנֵה, אֵל בְּנֵה, בְּנֵה בֵּיתְךָ בְּקָרוֹב.

טָהוֹר הוּא, יָחִיד הוּא, כַּבִּיר הוּא, לָמוּד הוּא, מֶלֶךְ הוּא נוֹרָא הוּא, סַגִּיב הוּא, עִזּוּז הוּא, פּוֹדֶה הוּא, צַדִּיק הוּא יִבְנֶה בֵּיתוֹ בְּקָרוֹב. בִּמְהֵרָה, בִּמְהֵרָה, בְּיָמֵינוּ בְּקָרוֹב. אֵל בְּנֵה, אֵל בְּנֵה, בְּנֵה בֵּיתְךָ בְּקָרוֹב.

קָדוֹשׁ הוּא, רַחוּם הוּא, שַׁדַּי הוּא, תַּקִּיף הוּא יִבְנֶה בֵּיתוֹ בְּקָרוֹב. בִּמְהֵרָה, בִּמְהֵרָה, בְּיָמֵינוּ בְּקָרוֹב. אֵל בְּנֵה, אֵל בְּנֵה, בְּנֵה בֵּיתְךָ בְּקָרוֹב.

אֶחָד מִי יוֹדֵעַ?

אֶחָד אֲנִי יוֹדֵעַ: אֶחָד אֱלֹהֵינוּ שֶׁבַּשָּׁמַיִם וּבָאָרֶץ.

שְׁנַיִם מִי יוֹדֵעַ? שְׁנַיִם אֲנִי יוֹדֵעַ: שְׁנֵי לֻחוֹת הַבְּרִית, אֶחָד אֱלֹהֵינוּ שֶׁבַּשָּׁמַיִם וּבָאָרֶץ.

שְׁלֹשָׁה מִי יוֹדֵעַ? שְׁלֹשָׁה אֲנִי יוֹדֵעַ: שְׁלֹשָׁה אָבוֹת, שְׁנֵי לֻחוֹת הַבְּרִית, אֶחָד אֱלֹהֵינוּ שֶׁבַּשָּׁמַיִם וּבָאָרֶץ.

אַרְבַּע מִי יוֹדֵעַ? אַרְבַּע אֲנִי יוֹדֵעַ: אַרְבַּע אִמָּהוֹת, שְׁלֹשָׁה אָבוֹת, שְׁנֵי לֻחוֹת הַבְּרִית, אֶחָד אֱלֹהֵינוּ שֶׁבַּשָּׁמַיִם וּבָאָרֶץ.

חֲמִשָּׁה מִי יוֹדֵעַ? חֲמִשָּׁה אֲנִי יוֹדֵעַ: חֲמִשָּׁה חוּמְשֵׁי תוֹרָה, אַרְבַּע אִמָּהוֹת, שְׁלֹשָׁה אָבוֹת, שְׁנֵי לֻחוֹת הַבְּרִית, אֶחָד אֱלֹהֵינוּ שֶׁבַּשָּׁמַיִם וּבָאָרֶץ.

שִׁשָּׁה מִי יוֹדֵעַ? שִׁשָּׁה אֲנִי יוֹדֵעַ: שִׁשָּׁה סִדְרֵי מִשְׁנָה, חֲמִשָּׁה חוּמְשֵׁי תוֹרָה, אַרְבַּע אִמָּהוֹת, שְׁלֹשָׁה אָבוֹת, שְׁנֵי לֻחוֹת הַבְּרִית, אֶחָד אֱלֹהֵינוּ שֶׁבַּשָּׁמַיִם וּבָאָרֶץ.

שִׁבְעָה מִי יוֹדֵעַ? שִׁבְעָה אֲנִי יוֹדֵעַ: שִׁבְעָה יְמֵי שַׁבַּתָּא, שִׁשָּׁה סִדְרֵי מִשְׁנָה, חֲמִשָּׁה חוּמְשֵׁי תוֹרָה, אַרְבַּע אִמָּהוֹת, שְׁלֹשָׁה אָבוֹת, שְׁנֵי לֻחוֹת הַבְּרִית, אֶחָד

Zemiros

אֱלֹהֵינוּ שֶׁבַּשָּׁמַיִם וּבָאָרֶץ.

שְׁמוֹנָה מִי יוֹדֵעַ? שְׁמוֹנָה אֲנִי יוֹדֵעַ: שְׁמוֹנָה יְמֵי מִילָה, שִׁבְעָה יְמֵי שַׁבַּתָּא, שִׁשָּׁה סִדְרֵי מִשְׁנָה, חֲמִשָּׁה חוּמְשֵׁי תוֹרָה, אַרְבַּע אִמָּהוֹת, שְׁלֹשָׁה אָבוֹת, שְׁנֵי לֻחוֹת הַבְּרִית, אֶחָד אֱלֹהֵינוּ שֶׁבַּשָּׁמַיִם וּבָאָרֶץ.

תִּשְׁעָה מִי יוֹדֵעַ? תִּשְׁעָה אֲנִי יוֹדֵעַ: תִּשְׁעָה יַרְחֵי לֵדָה, שְׁמוֹנָה יְמֵי מִילָה, שִׁבְעָה יְמֵי שַׁבַּתָּא, שִׁשָּׁה סִדְרֵי מִשְׁנָה, חֲמִשָּׁה חוּמְשֵׁי תוֹרָה, אַרְבַּע אִמָּהוֹת, שְׁלֹשָׁה אָבוֹת, שְׁנֵי לֻחוֹת הַבְּרִית, אֶחָד אֱלֹהֵינוּ שֶׁבַּשָּׁמַיִם וּבָאָרֶץ.

עֲשָׂרָה מִי יוֹדֵעַ? עֲשָׂרָה אֲנִי יוֹדֵעַ: עֲשָׂרָה דִבְּרַיָּא, תִּשְׁעָה יַרְחֵי לֵדָה, שְׁמוֹנָה יְמֵי מִילָה, שִׁבְעָה יְמֵי שַׁבַּתָּא, שִׁשָּׁה סִדְרֵי מִשְׁנָה, חֲמִשָּׁה חוּמְשֵׁי תוֹרָה, אַרְבַּע אִמָּהוֹת, שְׁלֹשָׁה אָבוֹת, שְׁנֵי לֻחוֹת הַבְּרִית, אֶחָד אֱלֹהֵינוּ שֶׁבַּשָּׁמַיִם וּבָאָרֶץ.

אַחַד עָשָׂר מִי יוֹדֵעַ? אַחַד עָשָׂר אֲנִי יוֹדֵעַ: אַחַד עָשָׂר כּוֹכְבַיָּא, עֲשָׂרָה דִבְּרַיָּא, תִּשְׁעָה יַרְחֵי לֵדָה, שְׁמוֹנָה יְמֵי מִילָה, שִׁבְעָה יְמֵי שַׁבַּתָּא, שִׁשָּׁה סִדְרֵי מִשְׁנָה, חֲמִשָּׁה חוּמְשֵׁי תוֹרָה, אַרְבַּע אִמָּהוֹת, שְׁלֹשָׁה אָבוֹת, שְׁנֵי לֻחוֹת הַבְּרִית, אֶחָד אֱלֹהֵינוּ שֶׁבַּשָּׁמַיִם וּבָאָרֶץ.

שְׁנֵים עָשָׂר מִי יוֹדֵעַ? שנים עשר אֲנִי יוֹדֵעַ: שְׁנֵים עָשָׂר שִׁבְטַיָּא, אַחַד עָשָׂר כּוֹכְבַיָּא, עֲשָׂרָה דִבְּרַיָּא, תִּשְׁעָה יַרְחֵי לֵדָה, שְׁמוֹנָה יְמֵי מִילָה, שִׁבְעָה יְמֵי שַׁבָּתָא, שִׁשָּׁה סִדְרֵי מִשְׁנָה, חֲמִשָּׁה חוּמְשֵׁי תוֹרָה, אַרְבַּע אִמָּהוֹת, שְׁלשָׁה אָבוֹת, שְׁנֵי לֻחוֹת הַבְּרִית, אֶחָד אֱלֹהֵינוּ שֶׁבַּשָּׁמַיִם וּבָאָרֶץ.

שְׁלשָׁה עָשָׂר מִי יוֹדֵעַ? שְׁלשָׁה עָשָׂר אֲנִי יוֹדֵעַ: שְׁלשָׁה עָשָׂר מִדַּיָּא. שְׁנֵים עָשָׂר שִׁבְטַיָּא, אַחַד עָשָׂר כּוֹכְבַיָּא, עֲשָׂרָה דִבְּרַיָּא, תִּשְׁעָה יַרְחֵי לֵדָה, שְׁמוֹנָה יְמֵי מִילָה, שִׁבְעָה יְמֵי שַׁבָּתָא, שִׁשָּׁה סִדְרֵי מִשְׁנָה, חֲמִשָּׁה חוּמְשֵׁי תוֹרָה, אַרְבַּע אִמָּהוֹת, שְׁלשָׁה אָבוֹת, שְׁנֵי לֻחוֹת הַבְּרִית, אֶחָד אֱלֹהֵינוּ שֶׁבַּשָּׁמַיִם וּבָאָרֶץ.

חַד גַּדְיָא, חַד גַּדְיָא

חַד גַּדְיָא, חַד גַּדְיָא דְּזַבִּין אַבָּא בִּתְרֵי זוּזֵי, חַד גַּדְיָא, חַד גַּדְיָא.

וְאָתָא שׁוּנְרָא וְאָכְלָה לְגַדְיָא, דְּזַבִּין אַבָּא בִּתְרֵי זוּזֵי, חַד גַּדְיָא, חַד גַּדְיָא.

וְאָתָא כַלְבָּא וְנָשַׁךְ לְשׁוּנְרָא, דְּאָכְלָה לְגַדְיָא, דְּזַבִּין אַבָּא בִּתְרֵי זוּזֵי, חַד גַּדְיָא, חַד גַּדְיָא.

וְאָתָא חוּטְרָא וְהִכָּה לְכַלְבָּא, דְּנָשַׁךְ לְשׁוּנְרָא, דְּאָכְלָה לְגַדְיָא, דְּזַבִּין אַבָּא בִּתְרֵי זוּזֵי, חַד גַּדְיָא, חַד גַּדְיָא.

וְאָתָא נוּרָא וְשָׂרַף לְחוּטְרָא, דְּהִכָּה לְכַלְבָּא, דְּנָשַׁךְ לְשׁוּנְרָא, דְּאָכְלָה לְגַדְיָא, דְּזַבִּין אַבָּא בִּתְרֵי זוּזֵי, חַד גַּדְיָא, חַד גַּדְיָא.

וְאָתָא מַיָּא וְכָבָה לְנוּרָא, דְּשָׂרַף לְחוּטְרָא, דְּהִכָּה לְכַלְבָּא, דְּנָשַׁךְ לְשׁוּנְרָא, דְּאָכְלָה לְגַדְיָא, דְּזַבִּין אַבָּא בִּתְרֵי זוּזֵי, חַד גַּדְיָא, חַד גַּדְיָא.

וְאָתָא תּוֹרָא וְשָׁתָה לְמַיָּא, דְּכָבָה לְנוּרָא, דְּשָׂרַף לְחוּטְרָא, דְּהִכָּה לְכַלְבָּא, דְּנָשַׁךְ לְשׁוּנְרָא, דְּאָכְלָה לְגַדְיָא, דְּזַבִּין אַבָּא בִּתְרֵי זוּזֵי, חַד גַּדְיָא, חַד גַּדְיָא.

וְאָתָא הַשּׁוֹחֵט וְשָׁחַט לְתוֹרָא, דְּשָׁתָה לְמַיָּא, דְּכָבָה לְנוּרָא, דְּשָׂרַף לְחוּטְרָא, דְּהִכָּה לְכַלְבָּא, דְּנָשַׁךְ לְשׁוּנְרָא, דְּאָכְלָה לְגַדְיָא, דְּזַבִּין אַבָּא בִּתְרֵי זוּזֵי, חַד גַּדְיָא, חַד גַּדְיָא.

וְאָתָא מַלְאַךְ הַמָּוֶת וְשָׁחַט לְשׁוֹחֵט, דְּשָׁחַט לְתוֹרָא, דְּשָׁתָה לְמַיָּא, דְּכָבָה לְנוּרָא, דְּשָׂרַף לְחוּטְרָא, דְּהִכָּה לְכַלְבָּא, דְּנָשַׁךְ לְשׁוּנְרָא,

דְּאָכְלָה לְגַדְיָא, דְּזַבִּין אַבָּא בִּתְרֵי זוּזֵי, חַד גַּדְיָא, חַד גַּדְיָא.

וְאָתָא הַקָּדוֹשׁ בָּרוּךְ הוּא וְשָׁחַט לְמַלְאַךְ הַמָּוֶת, דְּשָׁחַט לְשׁוֹחֵט, דְּשָׁחַט לְתוֹרָא, דְּשָׁתָה לְמַיָּא, דְּכָבָה לְנוּרָא, דְּשָׂרַף לְחוּטְרָא, דְּהִכָּה לְכַלְבָּא, דְּנָשַׁךְ לְשׁוּנְרָא, דְּאָכְלָה לְגַדְיָא, דְּזַבִּין אַבָּא בִּתְרֵי זוּזֵי, חַד גַּדְיָא, חַד גַּדְיָא.

IT IS AN appropriate end to the *Seder*, reaffirming what we're supposed to always believe but don't always see so well. Nothing is random. There is no such thing as coincidence. Everything is connected, and all of it points back to God. This is why we can say things like, "Everything is for the good."[1] It has to be because, "All that God does is for the good,"[2] especially when it comes to the Jewish people.

This is why there is also a custom to say *Shir HaShirim* at this point. *Shir HaShirim*, authored by the wisest man ever, Shlomo *HaMelech*, is the quintessential love song between God and the Jewish people. It is the depth of one's love for another that determines how deep their faith will be in each

---

[1] *Ta'anis* 21a.
[2] *Brochos* 60b.

other, and how hard each will fight to preserve the relationship.

There are many things in life that provide a person with joy, but most of that joy is limited and fleeting—except for love of God, the love a person feels *from* God, and the love they feel *for* Him. It is the spiritual blood that courses through a person, providing them with the life energy to survive and accomplish.

It was also the goal of the *Seder*. We tend to feel love for sincere goodness, especially when we have been the recipients of that good. After spending hours recounting all the good God did for our ancestors, of which we are the beneficiaries, we are primed to love God, for as the *Rambam* has said:

What is the process for coming to love and fear God? When one contemplates His actions and His wondrous and great creations and sees in them His wisdom, that it has no limit and no end, immediately he will love and praise Him, and desire tremendously to know His great Name. (*Yad Chazakah, Yesodei HaTorah*, 2:2)

If, after all we have done tonight, and even more so after all we have done in our lives, we immediately love and want to praise God and desire tremendously to know His great Name, we have justified our existence. And there is nothing more liberating than this.

Thank you for your contribution

Alvin & Yehudis Schamroth
Alain Bitton
Rene Levy
Susan Renee King
In honor of Adel Jacobs & Ushala Israel Jacobs

L'illuy Nishmas David ben Yael, Uriel Kalendarev (El-Gad), Ruslan "Russell" ben Bela & Isaac ben Emmoh

Chavatzelet Isaacson
David Shabat
Ithiel & Ruth Snyder
Robert Abraham
Steven & Naomi Weintraub

Denise Mordechai
Rachel Krantman

Thirtysix.org

Over 100 books on various different topics of Torah philosophy, including translations of some classical Kabbalistic works, available through www.thirtysix.org and Amazon.com.

Made in the USA
Columbia, SC
18 September 2024

6c4c7033-df56-4e1f-8124-e9d1dd3546f4R01